HAPPY
DAYS
EVERYDAY

HAPPY DAYS EVERYDAY

100 PRINCIPLES OF HAPPINESS WITH A 22 DAY TRANSFORMATION PROGRAM

MAKE QUANTUM JOYFUL LEAPS TODAY

CAESAR OSIRIS

Edit by Emily B
The Art Of Editing
Illustrations by Reitchiel
Cover design by Oyekola Sodiq Ajibola
Book design by Eugene Rijn Saratorio

Made in U.S.A.
Although every precaution has been taken in the preparation of this book, the publisher and author assume no responsibility for errors or omissions. Neither is any liability assumed for damages resulting from the use of information contained herein.

ISBN 978-1-7357808-8-7

TABLE OF CONTENT

TO YOU, I HOPE YOU MAKE QUANTUM JOYFUL LEAPS

INTRODUCTION

IN THE BEGINNING of our lives, when we are born, we are very curious about our environment and also our bodies. We are curious about what we see, what we touch and feel, and the flavors that either captivate us or disgust us. When we are just born, we have the capacity to become joyful and happy in less than a second because of the simplest things. At that age, we don't need that much to feel bliss, as long it is fun, we feel love and get nutrients. We are usually present and enjoy each moment to the point of expanding and bending time. When we are kids, we are free and unconsciously fearless to explore our limits while just having a good time. But then we start getting distracted with information learned from our parents or family, traumas, consuming cheap entertainment, or doing other unfertile practices that take us away from the initial instinct of knowing how to instinctively be present in mind-body-spirit.

We grow and get busy in life searching for success, for money, and all the elements that we were conditioned to believe we needed to thrive and just simply be happy, joyful! Life can be as fun and happy as it was when we were kids. We spend so much time after things, social status, that dream car or income, that house or watch, ignoring that within our body-mind-spirit we can find and create the reality we want. We forget that our energy-conscious is connected to the universal web of life, and we are the "observer-creator" of our own reality.

I've heard people say they have never been happy or others saying that their life was so hard that they don't feel emotions anymore. I have news for anyone who thinks that way, we all feel emotions, and we are all capable of transforming our emotions and creating massive changes in our lives while living the bliss of experiencing life on earth.

Most of the education that a child receives in school is not about how to deal with their emotions, or how to get to know their body or energy-consciousness. Kids don't learn about how to be happy in life, or how to cultivate positive thoughts and actions that will make your life fertile for success to grow.

With this book, you can take it as that class or workshop, or simply as a friend that is visiting you from afar and is sharing valuable information with you. A friend that is going to guide you on how to optimize your life towards happiness and take the joyful leap.

The best way to use the book is with a notebook or journal in which you will write, take notes, and answer the questions that you will find for each chapter along the way.

Self-help is actually about questioning things yourself; therefore, the "question" element in this self-help book will be very present. I hope these questions can help you generate new questions that will continue to inspire you to be constantly making the joyful leap.

At the end of each chapter, you will also find the principals of happiness, and there is a total of 100 of them. There are obviously more than 100 principals of happiness, I just chose to write 100, but I hope this book can help you to throughout your life finding more than one million principles, values, or ways of experiencing the bliss of life.

At the end of the book, you will find the 22-day transformation plan. It was created to jump-start someone's life to make the quantum leap towards happiness in 22 days or less. The goal of the 22-day plan is to create drastic positive disruption in your life, to completely change your body-mind-spirit environment so you can make the joyful leap. It includes Quantum Diets and Quantum Workouts that you will have to choose one of each to adopt during your 22-day transformation program. It will also guide you to develop the skill of self-discipline, creating new positive habits that will make your life fertile for joy and anything you want. At the end of the day it is up to you and your commitment to yourself on whether you will start living a new joyful reality through applying this information in your life.

To make joyful leaps is important to adapt to change, and this something that most people fear. We always hear people saying, "things are changing so much", because we think it is "natural" to have things remaining the same. But the nature of the world is that it is constantly changing and evolving. We need to normalize the idea of change; it is normal that things will change. Therefore, we must ground and stabilize our life by filtering our experiences with happiness so we can make joyful leaps.

PART I

BODY, MIND, AND SPIRIT

HEALTH IS HAPPINESS

> *Health is a state of complete harmony of the body, mind and spirit.*"
>
> – B.K.S. Iyengar

IMAGINE THAT HAPPINESS is a beautiful flower that grows out of a delicate plant that we all dream to possess. When you get a plant, there are three essential elements that the plant will need: soil, sun, and water. Without it, the plant can die. Now, imagine that the soil represents the mind-body-spirit health and that you are the gardener planting the seeds of happiness, joy, and peace.

The mind, body, and spirit are like fertile soil that anything grows in; whatever you plant on it will grow. If you plant positive emotions and thoughts, you will have a positive outcome. If you plant a poisoned seed, or a negative thought or emotion, a negative outcome will then grow in your soil.

Health is the foundation of a joyful life. But what exactly is health? Having a caesar salad for lunch with a diet coke? Drinking Gatorade or stevia?

Health is the ultimate expression of life; when your body-mind-spirit are in complete synchronicity and harmony with each other and the environment.

Maintaining a healthy lifestyle has both short and long-term health benefits. Long term, eating a balanced diet, taking regular exercise, and maintaining a healthy weight can add years to your life and reduce the risk of certain diseases including cancer, diabetes, cardiovascular disease, osteoporosis, and obesity.

We can avoid diseases by keeping an alkaline body, a clear mind, healthy and positive thoughts, a profound spiritual connection with yourself and your energy, and a healthy connection with nature and the otherness. Reducing the risks of diseases successfully can give you the stamina to go actively exploring the world, living a happy and joyful life. Sometimes diseases can bring sadness and even death, but keeping your body-mind-spirit connection is key to creating space for joy and happiness to grow.

In the short-term, health can also make you feel and look your best, give you more energy and glow. Your skin will look better, and your self-esteem and confidence will boost organically.

Making small changes to your daily life like eating healthier food, practicing a physical activity, practicing mindfulness, and taking more time to connect with your own wisdom and spirituality will create fertile soil for your joy to grow and expand. Improving your lifestyle with small steps in the right direction will have a big impact on your well-being, and real organic happiness and joy will manifest around you.

The one way you can take control of your health is by the awareness of your body-mind-spirit anatomy.

I have chosen to be happy because it is good for my health."
– Voltaire

ASK YOURSELF:

1. Am I cultivating a healthy lifestyle?
2. Which unhealthy habits do I have that prevent me from making the joyful leap?
3. Am I willing to do what it takes to improve my mind-body-spirit health? Why?
4. When was the last time I was being proactive with my health?
5. When was the last time I connected with the wisdom of my body?
6. Is there anything in my body that requires medical attention or healing?
7. What can I do to improve my health today?

8. Am I taking care of my heart and my mind?
9. Am I experiencing unhealthy or self-destructive thoughts that might require me to seek professional help?
10. How will I know I am being proactive with my health?

PRINCIPLE 1

Activate your mind-body-spirit health awareness.

SPIRIT ENERGY

The nature of universe is different from what we perceive and the matter as we see is just energy at the quantum level. Considering human body in the light of physics, we are energy beings."

— Anupama Garg

ENERGY IS LIFE. The energy is the spirit. The basic characteristics of energy from a scientific perspective is the capacity for any of its forms to undergo transformation to another.

Energy can be seen in many ways, but its basic manifestations will be kinetic, potential, or internal. Kinetic energy is the momentum possessed by anybody. Potential energy is the interactive potency of a system's component parts, whether the poles of a battery or the gravitational forces of the planets. Internal energy is held within molecules by the interactions of their atoms.

Each manifestation of energy is constantly transforming and changing its various states. Energy doesn't die; it transforms.

The energy in our body is constantly moving and transforming. From the energy we eat to the energy we use to move, even thoughts influence our energy.

We get energy from eating, from sleeping and the sun. From other people, bodies of waters like rivers, the ocean, and nature. Later on, we will explore the energy of foods and how it affects your body and your emotions, but what is important to know for now is that your spiritual energy is constantly changing and transforming. We can transform our energy by using it and releasing it. Any form of physical activity helps, any sports as long as you are active.

When we are aware of that, the fact that our energy is constantly changing, we can then purposefully transform it and align it to the energy of the truth we seek, or that idea of ourselves we want to manifest.

THE ENERGY-CONSCIOUSNESS

Through the findings of modern physics, such as the theory of relativity and quantum mechanics, we now understand the duality of matter-energy, time-space, and particle-wave. That matter and energy are interchangeable, that time and space are relative and connected, and that quantum events have the attributes of both particles and waves. One important relationship science has not yet resolved is between energy and consciousness. We do know that consciousness, which used to be considered a property or product of the individual brain of a sentient being, is involved in the manifestation of physical reality in the universe. Even though science can describe how consciousness exists or how it is woven into the fabric of the universe, it seems we cannot avoid consciousness if we are to explain physical reality in an integrative way.

But if we were to base our thoughts on the quantum mechanics theory that all matters are energy, we can assume that energy also possesses the consciousness.

The two primary aspects or components of reality that the universe reveals to us through these discoveries are energy and consciousness. All other things that are found in the universe can be understood as manifestations of these two fundamentals.

There are historical views that see these two as one. In the Eastern tradition, energy and consciousness are viewed as different aspects of the same thing. In this tradition, energy is understood to be the origin and reality of the universe. As seen in the ancient Taoist principle, that mind creates energy, and energy creates mind, energy, and mind are viewed as one inseparable entity. Energy and mind, while changing to each other and producing limitlessly diverse phenomena, are ultimately one.

The Vedic tradition of India teaches the same principle, using different terminology: silence and dynamism are together forever. SHIVA (silence, unbounded pure consciousness) and SHAKTI (dynamism, creativity) are always united in a cosmic embrace of wholeness that creates and sustains the world.

The fabric of the universe is made of energy-consciousness, and also what we know about reality is that it creates, sustains, and regulates the cosmos, called this 'energy-consciousness'.

According to Jung's teachings, the collective unconscious is common to all human beings and is responsible for a number of deep-seated beliefs and instincts, such as life and death instincts.

Your energy-consciousness is part of a bigger consciousness; what Jung calls the collective unconsciousness, and what Christians call the Holy Spirit or the God energy. We are all part of it.

You are aware of your own consciousness and aware of your body and needs, which gives you a sense of identity. You are a unique expression of the collective energy-conscious matter in the universe. You can explore the different rages of the frequency of that universal conscious-energy through the emotions that you are cultivating in your magnetic-sphere or body. Enlightenment, Peace & Joy being the highest frequency of that conscious energy. Connecting with those emotions will not only activate your energy unconsciously, but it will manifest in your life in a creative and expanding way. Your emotions are part of a higher collective god-energy-consciousness, and when you access them, you are connected to that universal force.

ASK YOURSELF:

1. When was the last time I felt I connected with my spirit-energy or energy-consciousness?
2. How can I improve the connection with my energy-consciousness today?
3. Is my energy sitting and not moving much? Are my thoughts feeling stuck?

4. Which physical activities can I adopt in my lifestyle to move my energy?
5. How can I improve my diet with a more alkaline diet that will support my energy?
6. Is my energy being affected by the frequency of positive or negative emotions?
7. Will I consider my energy-consciousness a happy one? Or what instead?
8. How will I know my energy-consciousness is in a healthy place?

PRINCIPLE 2

Connect with and activate your energy-consciousness.

PRINCIPLE 3

Connect with the universal energy-consciousness through high-frequency emotions.

THE BODY

WHEN WE ARE born, we don't have a clear idea of the boundaries of our body, as we don't really understand our body as an organism yet. Nonetheless, there is an instinctive way we connect with our bodies that fades out as we grow older and learn all these ideas we have about our bodies.

We continue to explore ourselves in the world through our bodies, and usually, when we become teenagers, when changes start to occur in our body is when we pay attention for the first time. Most of the time, our first approach is negative or unhealthy.

For example, when I was in my transition to becoming a teenager, I was overweight, and in order to avoid being subject of bullying, I decided to get more physically active and joined swimming classes and a soccer team. I have friends who became aware of their body for the first time when they found themselves overweight or injured, or comparing themselves to other teenagers, "too fat", "too short", "too tall", "too skinny", etc.

Even though I was swimming and practicing a sport, I wasn't really learning anything about my body. In the American school systems, at least, we learn about the body in a scientific way, but those curriculums are not designed for you to really understand and connect that information with your own body.

When I started college and initiated my acting curriculum, I needed to take dance classes and body awareness classes as part of the Theatre Department curriculum. There I met Viveca Vazquez & Petra Bravo, both dance teachers who really taught me and helped me to connect with my body for the first time in my entire life. It was a big eureka moment as I started recognizing and becoming aware of my skeleton, my muscles, my organs, my posture, my movement, and how emotions affected my body.

You might be thinking, what does my body have to do with my happiness and joy?

Your body is the host of your energy-consciousness, what you say or do to yourself, to your thoughts, they all have impactful repercussions in your body. This is because your body is made up of small atomic particles of energy-consciousness, that responds to how you feel, what you think and what you do.

Knowing and understanding how your happiness affects your body is the first thing we need to understand when it comes to fully integrating ourselves into a joyful lifestyle.

For example, you wouldn't be able to dance of happiness if your bones are not holding your body, and that is just one of the ways your body supports and even contributes to creating your happiness. Do you see how integrated your happiness is to your body now? First things, first: The Skeleton.

SKELETAL SYSTEM

The skeletal system works as a support structure for your body. It gives the body its shape, allows movement, and makes blood cells. The skeletal system's bones also protect internal organs, store calcium, and produce red and white blood cells.

The skeletal system is your body's central framework. It consists of bones and connective tissue, including cartilage, tendons, and ligaments. It's also called the musculoskeletal system. What does the skeletal system do?

SKELETAL SYSTEM

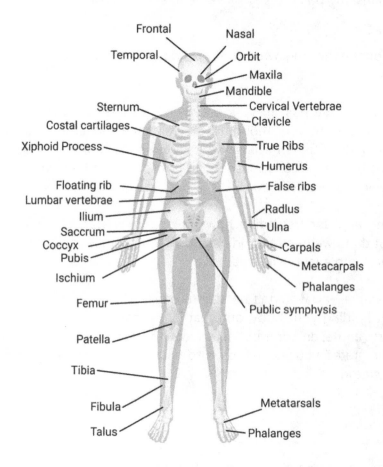

The skeletal system is a network of many different parts that work together to help you move. The main part of your skeletal system consists of your bones, which are hard structures that create your body's framework. There are 206 bones in an adult human skeleton. Each bone has three main layers:

1. **Periosteum:** The periosteum is a tough membrane that covers and protects the outside of the bone.
2. **Compact bone:** Below the periosteum, compact bone is white, hard, and smooth. It provides structural support and protection.

3. **Spongy bone:** The core, inner layer of the bone is softer than compact bone. It has small holes called pores to store marrow.

The other components of your skeletal system include:

1. **Cartilage:** This smooth and flexible substance covers the tips of your bones where they meet. It enables bones to move without friction (rubbing against each other). When the cartilage wears away, as in arthritis, it can be painful and cause movement problems.
2. **Joints:** A joint is where two or more bones in the body come together. There are three different joint types. The types of joints are:
- **Immovable joints:** Immovable joints don't let the bones move at all, like the joints between your skull bones.
- **Partly movable joints:** These joints allow limited movement. The joints in your rib cage are partly movable joints.
- **Movable joints:** Movable joints allow a wide range of motion. Your elbow, shoulder, and knee are movable joints.
3. **Ligaments:** Bands of strong connective tissue called ligaments hold bones together.
4. **Tendons:** Tendons are bands of tissue that connect the ends of a muscle to your bone.

To keep your skeletal system strong and healthy, you should:

- Get plenty of vitamin D and calcium in your diet.
- Drink plenty of water to help keep tissues healthy.
- Exercise regularly to strengthen bones and joints.
- Stay at a healthy weight to avoid putting extra pressure on your bones and cartilage.
- Wear protective gear during contact sports such as football and hockey.
- Be aware of your posture.

CONNECTING WITH THE SKELETON

We can control our posture. Sit upright and breathe naturally, even when watching TV. TV will rapidly become uninteresting.

The importance of having an accurate understanding of how the various parts of our body fit together lies in one of the basic tenets of the Alexander Technique work. I like to state it as,

"If you change what you think, you can change how you move. And if you change how you move, you will change what you feel."

Does that mean there is a connection between matter-energy-consciousness? – Absolutely!

By changing our conceptions of how our parts fit together, we can change how we move them and change how we feel. The accompanying feeling can be one of enormous relief and fascination with the wisdom underlying our creation.

What Alexander's work teaches us is that if we want to make a change, we need to rethink what we are doing so that the changed feeling is a result of the change in our way of moving. But also note that it is the nagging feeling that everything is not as we would like it that leads us to rethink what we are doing.

Thinking, feeling, and doing all have their useful function in our lives; in fact, it is necessary to use all three in a coordinated way if we don't want to get lost in any one of them. We need to learn how, when, and for what is best to use each of them.

One of my favorite quotes from F.M. Alexander comes from George Trevelyan's diary of his experiences on the first Alexander Technique teacher training course for Dec. 8, 1933:

> *We work to undo something and to feel out what change can be made. If we know beforehand what we are going to do we are lost. If the pupil does the thinking he will not slip back quite to the point he was before. But the trouble is*

none of my pupils will believe that all they need to do is to think and that wish for the neck to be free will do the trick. I could now with my hands make any alteration in anyone, but none will trust to the thought. We are so brutalized by our belief in doing and muscular tension."

The muscular system consists of three different types of muscles, including skeletal muscles, which are attached to bones by tendons and allow for voluntary movements of the body. Smooth muscle tissues control the involuntary movements of internal organs, such as the organs of the digestive system, allowing food to move through the system. Smooth muscles in blood vessels allow vasoconstriction and vasodilation helping regulate body temperature. Cardiac muscle tissues control the heart's involuntary beating, allowing it to pump blood through the blood vessels of the cardiovascular system.

CONNECTING WITH THE MUSCLES

If you look at the palm of one hand and then turn your palm away from your face, you will have made an obviously spiral-based movement that a lizard, for example, could not imitate. A slightly more complex example: starting from sitting, facing away from the door of the room, rise from the chair, turn and start to walk towards the door, all in one movement.

MUSCULAR SYSTEM

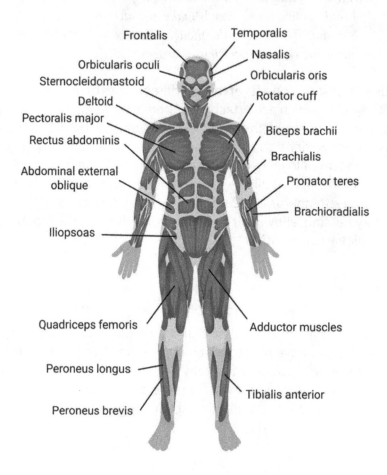

BODY CONNECTION

TISSUES IN ORGANS

Although organs consist of multiple tissue types, many organs are composed of the main tissue that is associated with the organ's major function and other tissues that play supporting roles. The main tissue may be unique to that specific organ. For example, the heart's main tissue is cardiac muscle, which performs the heart's major function of pumping blood and is, therefore, found only in the heart. The heart also includes nervous and connective tissues that are required for it to perform its major function. For example, nervous tissues control the beating of the heart, and connective tissues make up heart valves that keep blood flowing in just one direction through the heart.

VITAL ORGANS

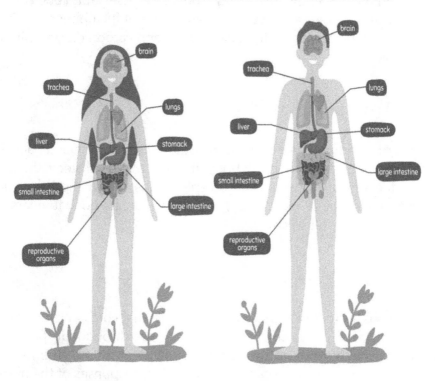

The human body contains five organs that are considered vital for survival. They are the heart, brain, kidneys, liver, and lungs. The locations of these five organs and several other internal organs are shown in the figure below. If any of the five vital organs stop functioning, the death of the organism is imminent without medical intervention.

1. The heart is located in the center of the chest, and its function is to keep blood flowing through the body. Blood carries substances to cells that they need and also carries away wastes from cells.
2. The brain is located in the head and functions as the body's control center. It is the seat of all thoughts, memories, perceptions, and feelings.
3. The two kidneys are located in the back of the abdomen on either side of the body. Their function is to filter blood and form urine, which is excreted from the body.
4. The liver is located on the right side of the abdomen. It has many functions, including filtering blood, secreting bile that is needed for digestion, and producing proteins necessary for blood clotting.
5. The two lungs are located on either side of the upper chest. Their main function is exchanging oxygen and carbon dioxide with the blood.

INTEGUMENTARY SYSTEM

Organs of the integumentary system include the skin, hair, and nails. The skin is the largest organ in the body. It encloses and protects the body and is the site of many sensory receptors. The skin is the body's first defense against pathogens, and it also helps regulate body temperature and eliminate wastes in sweat.

NERVOUS SYSTEM

The nervous system includes the brain and spinal cord, which make up the central nervous system, and nerves that run throughout the rest of the body, which make up the peripheral nervous system. The nervous system controls both voluntary and involuntary responses of the human organism and also detects and processes sensory information.

HUMAN NERVOUS SYSTEM

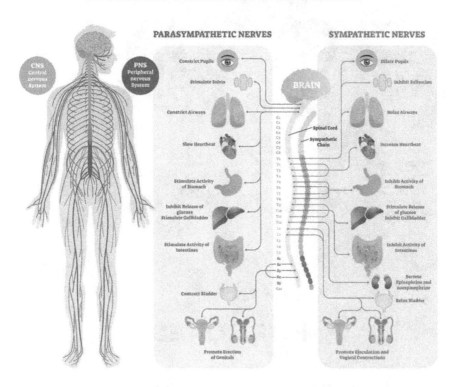

ENDOCRINE SYSTEM

The endocrine system is made up of glands that secrete hormones into the blood, which carries the hormones throughout the body. Endocrine hormones are chemical messengers that control many body functions, including metabolism, growth, and sexual development. The master gland of the endocrine system is the pituitary gland, which produces hormones that control other endocrine glands. Some of the other endocrine glands include the pancreas, thyroid gland, and adrenal glands.

Certain hormones are known to help promote positive feelings, including happiness and pleasure.

ENDOCRINE SYSTEM

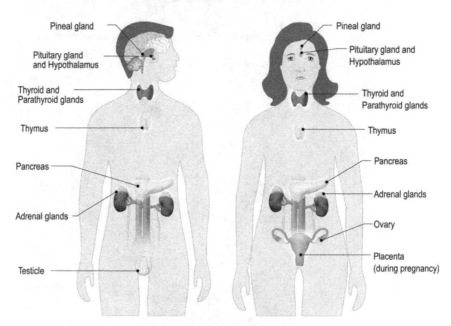

HORMONES

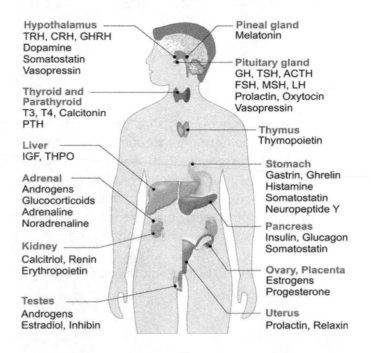

THE "HAPPY HORMONES":

1. DOPAMINE:

Known as the "feel good" hormone. This happy hormone is a neurotransmitter that drives your brain's reward system. If you are praised at work for doing a good job, you'll get a delicious dopamine hit, resulting in feelings of well-being. It also drives pleasure-seeking behavior. Boost it by setting realistic goals (e.g., tidying your desk or sticking to your workout schedule) and achieving them. And seek out pleasurable healthy activities that have a positive impact on your life.

2. SEROTONIN

This mood-boosting neurotransmitter was made famous by SSRI (selective serotonin reuptake inhibitor) antidepressants, which increase the brain's serotonin levels. The most effective and natural way to boost serotonin is by exercising daily; that's one reason a brisk walk does wonders for your mood.

3. OXYTOCIN

Both a neurotransmitter and a happy hormone, oxytocin is often called "the love hormone." Researchers from Claremont University in California have done extensive research on its impact on women, linking oxytocin release to life satisfaction levels. It may play a greater role in women's physiology and happiness compared to men's. Spending time with loved ones and being kind to others stimulates oxytocin. Don't you feel good just reading that?

4. ESTROGEN

This happy hormone helps form serotonin and protects you from irritability and anxiety, keeping your mood steady. Estrogen decreases with menopause, and lifestyle factors such as smoking and extreme exercise can also lower it. The estrogen/progesterone imbalance in perimenopause can also negatively affect mood. Stress management can balance them since stress hormones, such as cortisol, interfere with the secretion, action, and function of the two happy hormones.

5. PROGESTERONE

This helps you to sleep well and prevents anxiety, irritability, and mood swings.

Looking to boost your endorphins and serotonin levels? Spending time outdoors, in sunlight, is a great way to do this. According to the 2008 research by Trusted Source, exposure to sunlight can increase both serotonin and endorphins' production. Start with at least 10 to 15 minutes outside each day. If you're tired of the same old sights, try exploring a new neighborhood or park. Just don't forget the sunscreen!

There are several supplements that may help increase your happy hormone levels. Here are just a few to consider:

- Tyrosine (linked to dopamine production)
- Green tea and green tea extract (dopamine and serotonin)
- Probiotics (may boost serotonin and dopamine production)
- Tryptophan (serotonin)

Supplements may be helpful, but some aren't recommended for people with certain health conditions. They can also interact with certain medications, so make sure to talk to your healthcare provider before you try them.

If you do take any supplements, read all package instructions and stick to the recommended doses, since some can have negative effects at high doses.

Certain foods can also have an impact on hormone levels, so note the following when meal planning for a happy hormone boost:

- Spicy foods, which may trigger endorphin release
- Coconut yogurt, beans, and almonds are just a few foods linked to dopamine release
- Foods high in tryptophan, which have been linked to increased serotonin levels
- Foods containing probiotics, such as yogurt, kimchi, and sauerkraut, which can influence the release of hormones

CARDIOVASCULAR SYSTEM

The cardiovascular system (also called the circulatory system) includes the heart, blood, and three types of blood vessels: arteries, veins, and capillaries. The heart pumps blood, which travels through the blood vessels. The main function of the cardiovascular system is to transport. Oxygen from the lungs and nutrients from the digestive system are transported to cells throughout the body. Carbon dioxide and other waste materials are picked up from the cells and transported to organs such as the lungs and kidneys for elimination from the body. The cardiovascular system also equalizes body temperature and transports endocrine hormones to cells in the body where they are needed.

URINARY SYSTEM

The urinary system includes the pair of kidneys, which filter excess water and a waste product called urea from the blood and form urine. Two tubes called ureters carry the urine from the kidneys to the urinary bladder, which stores the urine until it is excreted from the body through another tube named the urethra. The kidneys also produce an enzyme called renin and a variety of hormones. These substances help regulate blood pressure, the production of red blood cells, and the balance of calcium and phosphorus in the body.

RESPIRATORY SYSTEM

Organs and other respiratory system structures include the nasal passages, lungs, and a long tube called the trachea, which carries air between the nasal passages and lungs. The respiratory system's main function is to deliver oxygen to the blood and remove carbon dioxide from the body. Gases are exchanged between the lungs and blood across the walls of capillaries lining tiny air sacs (alveoli) in the lungs.

LYMPHATIC SYSTEM

The lymphatic system is sometimes considered to be part of the immune system. It consists of a network of lymph vessels and ducts that collect excess fluid (called lymph) from extracellular spaces in tissues and transport the fluid to the bloodstream. The lymphatic system also includes many small collections of tissue, called lymph nodes, and an organ called the spleen, both of which remove pathogens and cellular debris from the lymph or blood. In addition, the thymus gland in the lymphatic system produces some types of white blood cells (lymphocytes) that fight infections.

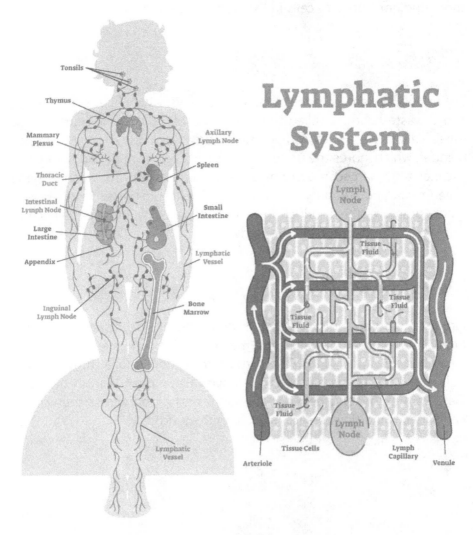

DIGESTIVE SYSTEM

The digestive system consists of several main organs — including the mouth, esophagus, stomach, and small and large intestines — that form a long tube called the gastrointestinal (GI) tract. Food moves through this tract where it is digested, its nutrients absorbed, and its waste products excreted. The digestive system also includes accessory organs (such as the pancreas and liver) that produce enzymes and other substances needed for digestion but through which food does not actually pass.

REPRODUCTIVE SYSTEM

The reproductive system is the only body system that differs substantially between males and females. Both male and female reproductive systems produce sex-specific sex hormones (testosterone in males, estrogen in females) and gametes (sperm in males, eggs in females). However, the organs involved in these processes are different. The male reproductive system includes the epididymis, testes, and penis, and the female reproductive system includes the uterus, ovaries, and mammary glands. The male and female systems also have different additional roles. For example, the male system has the role of delivering gametes to the female reproductive tract, whereas the female system has the roles of supporting an embryo and fetus until birth and also producing milk for the infant after birth.

INTAKE

What you ingest is very important for your body's well-being, especially what you eat and drink. For example, an alkaline diet will create the perfect circumstances for your body to work by keeping your body at the right PH level. The optimal PH of your blood should range between 7.35-7.45. The best way to test your PH and see if your body is in the optimal range is simple, go to your local health food store and but "PH strips", they are inexpensive and will provide you with a wonderful sense of relief and self-knowledge.

How to use it: when you wake up, spit out your first bunch of saliva, create a second batch of saliva in your mouth, and put the strip in. Just a couple seconds and it's done. Your morning saliva should be slightly under 7.3; if it is, you are good to go.

How would you know if you are on the acidic side of things? Well, for starters, you would have some acne on your body and possibly bad breath (halitosis). Another indicator of being more on the acid side is having heartburn.

Try to stick to foods that are great for alkalizing your system, such as most fruits and vegetables along with nuts and seeds. Drinking alkaline water, some stores sell 9.5, they are great. For acid foods, think of it this way, all dairy, meat most grains, and all foods that are packaged or canned are acidic for your body and create the perfect circumstances for diseases to take place in your body.

WAYS OF CONNECTING WITH YOUR BODY:

- Dancing and/or singing will immediately help you connect directly with your body in a fun way. I have a couple of albums that I slap on when I'm in the need for some feel-good time. The Polo & Pan is on the top of my happiness pile at the moment (and also what I'm listening to as I write this). Even though I can't carry a tune to save my life or bust a worthy move, this album gets me in the mood for relaxing and helps me come down from previously incalculable heights.
- Take a shower. This is one of my last-resort grounding methods. A hot shower can get things off of your skin, not mud or dirt, but bad thoughts, mad thoughts, misery, and stress. A hot shower is a perfect cure for this because it relaxes your tense muscles and literally washes it all off.
- Walk barefoot out in the park or nature. Shoes are great, but they really disconnect you from the earth beneath your feet. Recharge your energy and ground yourself while just walking barefoot out in nature.
- Gardening will help you connect with your body. It's not just your own garden that will bring you down to earth either; the

surrounding countryside is full of wildflowers and sometimes free food: wild fennel, hairy-bitter cress, wild garlic, chickweed, blackberries, samphire, and nettles. Gardening helps you breathe and re-appreciate the natural world around you.

- Moisturize and hydrate. With every glob of cream that you rub into your skin, you will feel reconnected with your body, which so often can feel unreal and alien to us.
- Practice a sport or physical discipline. Feeling strong is part of feeling good with your body.
- Give your body the best nutrients.
- Say good things to your body. Your body will listen to and react to everything you say to yourself and your body.

CONNECT WITH YOUR CELLS AND ATOMS

Connecting with your cells and atoms helps you operate as a whole. You are made of atoms, and your skin, muscles, and bones have cells. Stem cell regeneration gets your body to the "feeling good" space, and in the last part, there are a few cell generative diets that you can choose one to adopt and try.

ASK YOURSELF:

1. Do I know my body well enough to know how my emotions can affect it?
2. What physical activity can I adopt in my lifestyle that will help me connect with my body?
3. Am I giving the best nutrients to my body?
4. Do I have healthy practices with all my organs and body?
5. How will I know I am giving the best nutrients to my body?

PRINCIPLE 4

Become physically aware of your body.

PRINCIPLE 5

Move your body, dance, and sing.

PRINCIPLE 6

Stimulate your happy hormones with your diet.

PRINCIPLE 7

Practice a physical discipline.

PRINCIPLE 8

Moisturize, beautify, and nourish your body.

MOVEMENT

" I move, therefore I am."

– Hakuri Murakami

EXPLORING YOUR MOVEMENT is the most beautiful action and expression you can communicate non-verbally. Movement allows your body to do things, to be in action. It is important that you are aware of all your movements because that wisdom also translates to life itself.

RHYTHM

A rhythm is a magical tool inside our body, and we can all develop rhythm, we have it inside. Rhythm is part of your body in more ways than you imagine. Like the rhythm of your thoughts, the way you move your body, the rhythm of your words and sounds, the rhythm of your eyesight, your breathing. The way you touch your hair and open your eyes.

Explore your rhythms. Listen to your favorite song and just dance! Free yourself! Dance, dance, dance until you feel a trance-like joyful feeling in the way you move. Let the movements reveal to you. There is no judgment, and nobody cares! Move and shake that body!

HAPPINESS COMES FROM MOVEMENT

When you explore movement, you will find that some movements will spark thoughts, emotions, or ideas that will elevate your life, making joyful leaps.

41

FIND YOUR HAPPY MOVES!

ASK YOURSELF:

1. When was the last time you connected with your movement?
2. Have you ever let your body speak through movement?
3. When was the last time you danced?
4. How did it feel?
5. When was the last time you let the non-verbal expression of your body manifest to you?
6. How many new movements can you express today?

PRINCIPLE 9

Move with an intention.

PRINCIPLE 10

Explore your own rhythm and movement.

THE MIND

I F THE SPIRIT is the energy-consciousness, the mind is responsible for one's thoughts and feelings, the seat of the faculty of reason or the aspect of intellect and thought, perception, memory, emotion, will, and imagination, including all unconscious cognitive processes. The term is often used to refer, by implication, to the thought processes of reason.

Prioreschi (1996) concluded that by the end of the 5th century B.C., the question of whether the heart or the brain was the seat of intelligence remained unresolved in Western medicine. This changed with the works of Hippocrates (ca. 460 BC–ca. 370 BC), 'a figure of heroic proportions even if dimmed by the mist of time.' Hippocrates' oft-quoted statements show a clear understanding of the role of the brain vis-à-vis or relation to the mind:

> *Men ought to know that from the brain, and from the brain alone, arise our pleasures, joys, laughter and jests, as well as our sorrow, pains, griefs and tears, through it, in particular, we think, see hear and distinguish the ugly from the beautiful, the bad from the good, the pleasant from the unpleasant... I hold that the brain is the most powerful organ of the human body... Wherefore I assert that the brain is the interpreter of consciousness...*
> – Hippocrates on the sacred disease
> Quoted by Prioreschi [1996])

Therefore, the mind-brain is the interpreter of consciousness- energy, that is in you and shared collectively. That is why two people can be thinking the same information at the same time. Because the thought or information exists in a quantum level, and our mind digests it for us, and also translate what we experience through our senses into a cognitive state that becomes part of our consciousness.

In talking of the brain as an organ, Hippocrates very clearly refers to those functions which we ordinarily include in our understanding of the 'mind.' He talks of emotive mental functions like awareness, pleasures, understanding of emotions; cognitive mental functions like thinking and seeing; aesthetic mental functions like distinguishing the ugly from the beautiful, the pleasant from the unpleasant and ethical functions like distinguishing the bad from the good–all these as attributes of the brain, and brain alone. By which he really makes a clear connection between mental functions as we understand them ('mind') and the structure that produces it (brain).

The brain is the organ of the mind just as the lungs are the organs for respiration, but scientific research finds more and more evidence that our mind is also in all of our organs and not just the brain.

The mind is a virtual entity, one that reflects the workings of the neural networks, chemical, and hormonal systems in our brain. The mind cannot be localized to particular areas within the brain, though the entire cerebral cortex and deep grey matter form important components. Consciousness, perception, behavior, intelligence, language, motivation, drive, the urge to excel, and reasoning of the most complex kind are the product of the extensive and complex linkages between the different parts of the brain. Likewise, abnormalities attributed to the mind, such as the spectrum of disorders dealt with by psychiatrists and psychologists, are consequences of widespread abnormalities, often in the chemical processes within different parts of the brain.

It is important we take care of our mind, and if you find an atypical behavior in your thought patterns, you should seek professional help. Getting exercise, sleeping well, having a balanced diet, getting sunlight are some of the ways you can improve your brain health.

ASK YOURSELF:

1. Am I getting enough sleep?
2. Are my thoughts healthy?
3. How can I improve my mind functioning and health today?
4. When was the last time I rested my mind?
5. Are my thoughts stimulating my happiness?
6. What kind of thoughts am I creating that are stopping me from being happy and feeling fulfilled in life?
7. Do I have negative thought patterns about my own outcome? When did I start to believe that?
8. Which positive thoughts do I need to experience more in my mind-consciousness?
9. How will I know my thoughts are healthy and aligned with my purpose?

PRINCIPLE 11

Positive thoughts will create a positive outcome.

MINDFULNESS

> " *Be happy in the moment, that's enough. Each moment is all we need, not more.* "
>
> – Mother Theresa

MINDFULNESS IF THE quality of being conscious or aware of something, in other words being fully present in all moments. The key is that mindfulness is not only practiced during sitting meditation but in your everyday actions, as a matter of fact, I am not necessarily the kind of guy who will sit down to meditate. I am more inclined to being in a constant state of meditation practicing mindfulness, moving, and also articulating information through movement. We must be aware of our thoughts and what we are doing each moment. Deepak Chopra describes mindfulness saying that,

> " The awareness of a thought is not a thought."
>
> – Deepak Chopra

We begin by practicing mindfulness of the breath. If it is going in, we silently say "in" or become aware of it. If it is going out, we silently say, "out." That is the first step.

Then add being aware of what you are doing. Right now, as I write, the word on my breath is "writing" and "dancing".

If we add awareness of our thoughts and feelings, then doing useless things becomes really difficult, and that is a good thing. Also, we will become aware of negative thoughts or negative emotions, making it easy for us to snap out of it as we are seeing it coming. Then, when you can master that, you can bring awareness of the feelings and thoughts of the people around you.

HOW TO PRACTICE MINDFULNESS

Becoming more aware of where you are and what you're doing, without becoming overly reactive or overwhelmed by what's going on around you.

Mindfulness is a natural quality that we all have, and we can achieve it by "creating space". It's available to us in every moment if we take the time to appreciate it. When we practice mindfulness, we're practicing the art of creating space for ourselves, space between our thoughts, space to breathe, space between ourselves and our reactions. When you are in that "space" of mindfulness, expectations vanish.

You don't need to buy anything. You can practice anywhere; there's no need to go out and buy a special cushion or bench; all you need is to devote a little time and space to access your mindfulness skills every day.

There's no way to quiet your mind. That's not the goal here. It is not about quieting your mind. There's no bliss state or otherworldly communion. All you're trying to do is pay attention to the present moment, without judgment, almost like an observer. Sounds easy, right? Your mind will wander. As you practice paying attention to what's going on in your body and mind at the present moment, you'll find that many thoughts arise. Your mind might drift to something that happened yesterday, meander to your to-do list, our mind will try to be anywhere but where you are. But the wandering mind isn't something to fear, it's part of human nature, and it provides the magic moment for the essential piece of mindfulness practice, the piece that researchers believe leads to healthier, more agile brains: the moment when you recognize that your mind has wandered and fallen into negative thoughts.

If you notice that your mind has wandered, then you can consciously bring it back to the present moment, and you will find reason in the present moment to be grateful, happy, and in peace. The more you do this, the more likely you are to be able to do it again and again. And that beats walking around on autopilot any day (getting to your destination without remembering the drive, finding yourself with your hand in the bottom of a chip bag you only meant to snack a little from, etc.).

Your judgy brain will try to take over. The second part of the puzzle is the "without judgment" part. We're all guilty of listening to the critic in our heads a little more than we should. (That critic has saved us from disaster quite a few times.) But, when we practice investigating our judgments and diffusing them, we can learn to choose how we look at things and react to them. When you practice mindfulness, try not to judge yourself for whatever thoughts pop up. Notice judgments arise, make a mental note of them (some people label them "thinking"), and let them pass, recognizing the sensations they might leave in your body, and letting those pass as well.

It's all about returning your attention again and again to the present moment. It seems like our minds are wired to get carried away in thought, especially since we are hyper bombarded by information in our phones, computer, media, etc. That's why mindfulness is the practice of returning, again and again, to the breath. We use the sensation of the breath as an anchor to the present moment. And every time we return to the breath, we reinforce our ability to do it again.

While mindfulness might seem simple, it's not necessarily all that easy. The real work is to make time every day just to keep doing it. Here's a short practice to get you started:

- **Take a seat.** Find a place to sit that feels calm and quiet to you.
- **Set a time limit**. If you're just beginning, it can help to choose a short time, such as 5 or 10 minutes.
- **Notice your body.** You can sit in a chair with your feet on the floor, you can sit loosely cross-legged, in lotus posture, you can kneel, all are fine. Just make sure you are stable, and in a position that you can stay in for a while.
- **Feel your breath.** Follow the sensation of your breath as it goes out, and as it goes in.
- **Notice when your mind has wandered.** Inevitably, your attention will leave the sensations of the breath and wander to other places. When you get around to noticing this, in a few seconds, a minute, five minutes, simply return your attention to the breath.
- **Be kind to your wandering mind.** Don't judge yourself or obsess over the content of the thoughts you find yourself lost in. Just come back.

That's it! That's the practice. You go away, you come back, and you try to do it as kindly as possible. The ultimate goal is that you can practice mindfulness all the time, every day in any situation you are in. The more you practice mindfulness, the more it will become part of your thought process and lifestyle.

ASK YOURSELF:

1. How does my breathing go?
2. How does it sound?
3. Can I hear the ocean waves in my breathing?
4. How does my body feel?
5. How can I remember to reconnect with my breath to ignite my state of mindfulness?
6. Am I breathing from my diaphragm or my chest?
7. What am I seeing?
8. What is in front of me?
9. What am I feeling and thinking?
10. Looking at my emotions and thoughts from a distance, what new perspective can I find?
11. Which emotions are the people around me feeling?
12. How can I optimize the possibilities of this present time I am on? How can I optimize my fun, my happiness, and joy in this very present moment?

PRINCIPLE 12

Practice Mindfulness and create space.

PART II

THE EMOTIONAL FOUNDATION

EMOTIONAL INTELLIGENCE

We define emotional intelligence as the subset of social intelligence that involves the ability to monitor one's own and others' feelings and emotions, to discriminate among them and to use this information to guide one's thinking and actions."

– Salovey and Mayer

FROM EVEN BEFORE we are born at the hospital, we are already experiencing what some people consider the catalyst of life: emotions. These sentiments are part of our subjective state of mind. Emotions are biological states associated with the nervous system with behavioral responses or internal stimuli such as thoughts, memories, and feelings related to events that occur in our consciousness or environment.

Emotional intelligence is like our natural emotional radar that allows us to monitor our own emotions and the ones from those around us. With the information we gather from our emotional radar, we can guide our thoughts and even influence other people's thoughts and behavior positively. It also helps to recognize when someone else is experiencing toxic emotions, allowing us to become aware of it and not let it influence our own emotions.

Emotions and moods are different from each other. A mood is a state of mind that predisposes our reactions, and an emotion is more physical-chemical. For example, someone in a "bad" mood is more likely to feel annoyed and irritated if they trip on a misplaced object. Someone in a "good" mood is more likely to feel amused by the incident. In general, emotions are biological and phycological reactions to an event, while moods are present before and throughout the event.

Emotions by themselves are neither good nor bad. They are simply biological reactions. However, the way we think and act (or don't act) on our emotions can strongly affect our well-being and our happiness. The most important way we can be in harmony with our emotions is when we develop emotional intelligence. We can develop it by simply being aware of our emotions and the emotions of others.

Now, in order to achieve emotional awareness so that we can lead our emotions towards joy, it is important to know them, to categorize them, and to recognize them. Because emotions are subjective, people often disagree on how to categorize them. Some people claim humans only have six basic emotions. Others argue we have up to 34,000 unique types of feelings.

The educational system doesn't really teach us anything about our emotions when understanding them is one of the greatest achievements we can have in life. Neither our parents teach us about emotions; in fact, in some cases, it is precisely because of our parents that we are carrying negative emotional patterns that obstruct our own happiness. My first formal introduction to the emotional world was through acting techniques and theatre. It is no secret that actors work on their craft by developing emotional intelligence. Part of their work is becoming an emotional chameleon and being able to access a wide range of emotions in a conscious way. It takes practice to an actor to successfully truly be at the service of the emotions, but once the emotions are channeled, the truth is being delivered.

Just like the actor works on his craft to become a convicting storyteller, we all have to work in our emotional well-being to tell our story the way we want, with happiness and joy. Working our emotional craft requires to understand the emotional state beyond the shallow levels of any preconceived idea. So, let's dig right into it. How many emotions are there? Where are the emotions located in our bodies?

Alan S. Cowen and Dacher Keltner, Ph.D. from the University of California, Berkeley, identified 27 distinct categories of emotions. And here they are, by alphabetical order and not desirability, value or importance:

1. **Admiration** – Delighted approval and liking. A favorable judgment resulting in trust.
2. **Adoration** – The act of glorification of someone or something through deep love.
3. **Aesthetic Appreciation** – to be fully aware of the visual value of something or someone with deep gratitude.
4. **Amusement** – A feeling of delight at being entertained.
5. **Anxiety** – A state of worry and nervousness, resulting in compulsive behavior.
6. **Awe** – An overwhelming feeling of respect for someone or something.
7. **Awkwardness** – The quality of an embarrassing situation caused by unskilful, worried, inelegant, and ungraceful actions.
8. **Boredom** – An unsatisfactory and fatigued state of mind.
9. **Calmness** – Experiencing a relaxed state of mind by the absence of agitation or excitement.
10. **Confusion** – A mistake that results from misjudgment, ignorance, inattention, or lack of clarity.
11. **Craving** – An overwhelming desire for a particular thing.
12. **Disgust** – Strong feelings of repugnance and dislike.
13. **Empathic Pain**– A mental ability that allows one person to understand someone else's struggles, emotions, and state of mind.
14. **Entrancement** – Being delighted while filled with wonder and enchantment.
15. **Envy** – A feeling of discontented or resentful longing aroused by someone else's possessions, qualities, or luck.
16. **Excitement** – A feeling of intense emotional elevation.
17. **Fear** – The anticipation of some specific pain, failure, success, or danger with a strong desire to give up, feeling restrained, or wanting to avoid and run away.
18. **Horror** – Intense aversion and repulsion caused by a strong dislike of something or someone.
19. **Interest** – A sense of curiosity about a thing or person.
20. **Joy** – A feeling of expansion and freedom caused by a positive stimulus with desirable consequences.
21. **Nostalgia** – A longing for something past.
22. **Romance** – Talking or behaving amorously towards an idea, something, or someone.

23. **Sadness** – The quality of excessive mournfulness, unhappiness, and uncheerfulness.
24. **Satisfaction** – Gratification for the quality of life and the accomplishment of desired experiences.
25. **Sexual desire** – An overwhelming sexual attraction to someone.
26. **Sympathy** – Sharing the feelings and emotions with affinity or harmony between two people or more.
27. **Triumph** – A successful ending of a struggle or to reach goals.

Did you notice that Happiness didn't make it to the list? Well, it turns out that happiness is not an emotion. Professors, psychologists, and other professionals of the emotional spectrum have debated for years whether or not happiness is an emotion. The truth is that happiness is closer to being a mood, a filter, a perspective, then an emotion. We will be elaborating more about that later on.

Another common way to categorize emotions is through Dr. Robert Plutchik's emotion wheel. Plutchik arranges the eight basic emotions in a rainbow wheel. Each emotion is placed directly across from its "opposite", like so:

1. Joy vs. Sadness
2. Trust vs. Disgust
3. Fear vs. Anger
4. Surprise vs. Anticipation

According to Plutchik, many feelings are simply stronger or weaker versions of the eight basic emotions. For instance, rage is a more intense type of anger, while annoyance is a milder type. More complex emotions can be created by combining the eight basic emotions. For example, blending joy and trust or admiration together can create love.

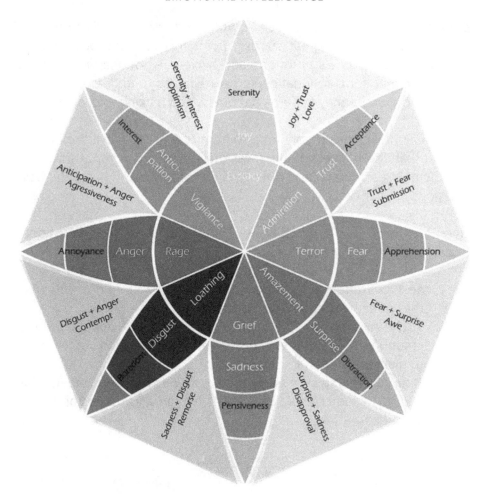

There are two ways to use the wheel, either as a two-dimensional circle or a three-dimensional ellipse. Utilizing it as a two-dimensional circle lets the individual dive into the emotion wheel. This can help anyone to discover the primary emotions they are feeling, as well as how emotions combine to create secondary emotions like awe, remorse, aggression, optimism, etc.

When utilizing it as a three-dimensional form, the individual can view the emotional intensity of the primary and secondary emotions (Roeckelein, 2006).

There are big differences between Plutchik's, and the 27 emotions from the Proceedings of National Academy of Sciences. Also, Plutchick's wheel does not express emotions, such as pride and shame. Aside from that, these tools provide a great starting point for detecting and igniting the awareness of one's emotions and achieve emotional intelligence. That is the emotional foundation someone needs to understand before embarking their journey towards happiness and making joyful leaps.

Emotional intelligence is very important in order to achieve the bliss of life, but that doesn't mean that logical intelligence is less important. They complement each other, and both intelligences help you make the best decisions in your capacity.

Here are three attributes that will help you train your Emotional Intelligence:

1. **Self-awareness** – You recognize your own emotions and how they affect your thoughts, behavior, and others.
2. **Social Awareness** – You have empathy. You can understand the emotions, needs, and concerns of other people, and you are able to pick up emotional cues.
3. **Animals or Nature Awareness** – Yes, you also have empathy for another living creature that is not human and understand their emotions and needs.

ASK YOURSELF:

1. How am I feeling?
2. What emotions am I experiencing?
3. What's taking up most of my headspace?
4. How is that making me feel?
5. When did I last eat a whole meal?
6. Am I tired?
7. What can I do today to experience happiness and bring Joy to my life?

PRINCIPLE 13

Practice Emotional Intelligence.

WHY DO WE HAVE EMOTIONS?

"Emotions can get in the way or get you on the way."
— Mavis Mazhura

THROUGHOUT HISTORY, PHILOSOPHERS have pondered whether humans truly benefit from having emotions or not. There are many cases in which strong emotional clouds our judgments make us do things we later regret. Would it not be better to operate purely on logic to survive? Logical and critical thinking are also very important, and developing both intelligences can help us thrive in life in a healthy and balanced way. However, emotions have a stronger impact on our consciousness and energy field because they are also part of the energy-consciousness.

In the past, our emotions motivated us toward certain survival strategies. Each basic emotion had its own purpose. For example, when our ancestors encountered a dangerous animal, fear prompted them to run away to safety. If they encountered an obstacle on their way home, anger motivated them to get rid of the problem instead of giving up. And upon arriving safely at home, feelings of joy would reinforce the behaviors that aided our ancestors' survival.

Our bodies' emotions are controlled and interpreted by a group of brain structures called the limbic system.

Limbic system

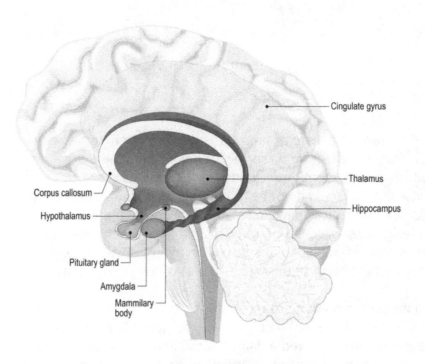

The limbic system releases chemicals that spur on our emotional states. The type of emotion we feel depends on which chemicals have been released. For example, the hormone oxytocin allows us to experience feelings of love and happiness.

RELAX YOUR BODY-MIND-SPIRIT

Emotions not only reflect our mental states or energetic state—but they also alter our body chemistry and nervous system functioning. For example, when we feel fear, our **Sympathetic Nervous System** activates. Our pupils dilate, our heart rate goes up, and we may start sweating. When a deer is being chased by a jaguar it's responding from the Sympathetic Nervous System.

Most people are in survival mode and taking actions from their Sympathetic nervous system. Let me give you a simple explanation of the difference between the sympathetic nervous system and the parasympathetic nervous system. They are very easy to remember and important to know when you are in both. Whenever you have a situation that puts you in stress, could be traffic, an argument with a partner, a noise in the middle of the night, etc., your body immediately turns on the switch to the Sympathetic nervous system. It means get out, get moving, there could be danger. Your blood starts flowing faster, and your digestion system turns off, eating, and drinking is the last thing your body wants to do.

During the parasympathetic time, your body will eat and digest food perfectly. You will sleep and dream, your cortisol levels will go down, and you may even lose some unwanted weight around your stomach. It is important to recognize when you are in either of the systems.

That's when practicing mindfulness can affect our emotions and our body. For example, if you are angry, afraid, or anxious, you can bring the awareness to your lungs, take deep breaths, and activate the **Parasympathetic Nervous System**. This system slows your heart rate and helps you calm down. Most of the time, we unconsciously activate our **Parasympathetic Nervous System** feeling safe, calmed, and aware. Therefore, always remember to breathe, breathe, and breathe.

That said, there are times in which emotions cause more problems than they solve. People with clinical anxiety may become paralyzed by fear rather than motivated by it. Individuals with depression can feel so much sadness that they lose the ability to feel joy, and isn't the world becoming more and more of this? Even people without clinical diagnoses can become overwhelmed with emotions.

In many cases, a compassionate counselor can help individuals control distressing emotions. In therapy or through self-help guidance like this book, individuals can learn how to recognize when feelings are clouding their judgment and bring those emotions down to a manageable level.

If intense emotions are affecting your ability to enjoy life and experience the bliss, you should find a counselor to help you understand your emotions. But if you choose to do the self-help way, it is important you practice the understanding of the root cause of your emotions: survival behavioral patterns.

According to Plutchik's Sequential Model, emotions are activated due to specific stimuli, which set off certain behavioral patterns.

He identified the following survival behaviors that drive our emotions and actions:

- **Protection:** Withdrawal, retreat (activated by fear and terror)
- **Destruction:** Elimination of barrier to the satisfaction of needs (activated by anger and rage)
- **Incorporation:** Ingesting nourishment (activated by acceptance)
- **Rejection:** Riddance response to harmful material (activated by disgust)
- **Reproduction:** Approach, contract, genetic exchanges (activated by joy and pleasure)
- **Reintegration:** Reaction to loss of nutrient product (activated by sadness and grief)
- **Exploration:** Investigating an environment (activated by curiosity and play)
- **Orientation:** Reaction to contact with an unfamiliar object (activated by surprise)

This means that when our emotions are activated, they are done so to elicit one of the survival behaviors. Of course, all of this happens on a subconscious level. I decided to organize it in my head so I could understand it. Using acting techniques as a reference, I found that there are Five Main Elements of Behaviour. The root of The Five Elements of behavior is always the Survival Behaviour and like a domino effect affecting, one by one, emotions, psychological reactions, physical reactions, and actions in that order.

THE FIVE ELEMENTS OF BEHAVIOR

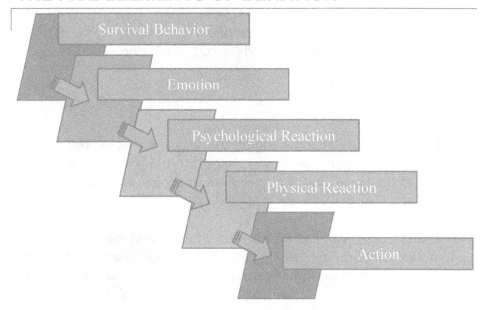

1- **Survival Behavior**

This is where an individual simply experiences the survival behaviors that drive their actions. You can use Plutchik's Sequential Model to identify it.

2- **Emotion**

This is where an individual simply experiences the emotion. It's about monitoring the internal universe and recognizing what is being experienced at each specific time.

3- **Psychological Reaction**

We react to the emotion with thoughts of what is happening to us. This component supports all others and is the chemical reaction that our body experiences. Our emotions are activated, and our mind is processing the information in order to bring sense into the narrative of each individual.

4- **Physical Reaction**

This where our body reacts to our emotions and thoughts. For instance, the rush of blood flow to the hands occurs when one experiences the emotion of anger.

5- **Action**

The chemical-physical reaction triggers the action. This is the response to a circumstance. It can be saying something, moving your body, adjusting the tone of the voice, making a decision, or simply doing any physical activity aligned with your intention.

With this diagram, you can locate your emotion and identify to which survival behavior you are responding to. By bringing mindfulness and self-awareness to your thoughts and emotions, you will be able to transform them, align them with your purpose and values before your actions. In other words, being aware of the 5 Elements of Behavior will help you intersect your own emotions and regenerate the emotions you want.

Earlier, we were talking about how Scientifics, Psychologists, and other mental health professionals don't consider happiness an emotion, and the answer is because happiness is a perspective.

Emotions are expressions of our consciousness, yet at the same time, they are the engine of our energy-consciousness. The emotions can affect the consciousness in a positive or negative way, raising the consciousness or degrading it.

Practicing mindfulness and emotional intelligence is a task that anyone aiming to live a happy and joyful life should implement in their lives in order to experience it from an elevated level of consciousness. If you are reading this, I suppose you are interested in elevating your journey towards a higher emotional consciousness, and I salute you as the world now more than ever needs more people like you.

But you're probably asking yourself, how do I know if my energy-consciousness is resonating at a higher or lower frequency at this very moment? The answer is again in your emotions. Each emotion has a frequency which becomes your metaphysical identity.

ASK YOURSELF:

1. What is my current operating survival mechanism?
2. What are my current 5 elements of behavior?
3. How does that make me feel?
4. Which emotion do I want to feel instead?
5. Am I operating from the Sympathetic Nervous system?
6. What would need to happen in my life for me to operate from my Parasympathetic Nervous System?
7. In which moments of my life have I operated from the Sympathetic Nervous System?
8. How will I know I am calmed and centered emotionally?
9. What actions should I take today regarding this matter that will bring joy and happiness to my life?

PRINCIPLE 14

Develop the awareness of The Elements of your Behavior.

PRINCIPLE 15

Breathe to activate your Parasympathetic Nervous System.

EMOTIONAL FREQUENCIES

> *Emotional intelligence is the ability to sense, understand, and effectively apply the power and acumen of emotions as a source of human energy, information, connection, and influence."*
>
> -Robert K. Cooper, PhD

Do you know what a magnet is? Magnets attract metallic shards or pieces of matter that hold metal in them. If you were to drag that magnet through a pile of sand, objects that are attracted to it by magnetism would stick to it. Not all of the sand would stick to it because not everything is attracted to it. Do you see how this works?

This concept also holds true for your life, emotions, and energy-consciousness. Your existence is based upon what matters to you. What is attracted to you in your life is based upon the energy or frequency that you emit, and likened energy frequencies are attracted back to you. This is how the universe works, it is also known as the law of attraction.

Do you remember thinking about someone, with an active unconscious emotion, and suddenly that persons text you, called you or sent you an email? That happens because we are connected energetically to each other, and emotions can also navigate an energy field with their own frequency.

To understand how vibrations and frequencies work, we first have to start by talking about energy. What is energy exactly? Energy is everything; everything is made of energy. Whether it be a plant, an object, a rock, a human, a dog, everything is part of an interconnected web of electromagnetic vibrational frequencies. This web of energy is commonly referred to as the "grid", a "life force" or "soul" that connects a stream of consciousness between all atoms and particles of the universe.

Vibrations refer to the oscillating and vibrating movement of atoms and particles caused by energy. Even solid objects like tables are actually made up of macroscopic vibrating atoms that receive, store, and emit energy. That is why humans and even our emotions have their own vibrational frequencies.

Frequencies are measured in hertz (Hz) units, which is the rate at which vibrations and oscillations occur. A frequency describes the number of waves that pass a fixed place in a given amount of time. Usually, a frequency is measured in the hertz unit, named in honor of the 19th-century German physicist Heinrich Rudolf Hertz. The hertz measurement, abbreviated Hz, is the number of waves that pass by per second.

Frequencies are used to determine and differentiate vibrational patterns. So, an atom that is vibrating at a faster rate would be considered a higher frequency than one that is vibrating at a much slower rate. Differentiating between high and low frequencies is important for understanding how the two interact with each other and can be beneficial or detrimental to our well-being and, of course, our happiness.

Different organs of the human body produce different resonance frequencies. The heart resonance frequency is 1 Hz. The brain has a resonance frequency of 10 Hz, blood circulation about 0.05 to 0.3 Hz, and so on.

Scientists from the National Research Nuclear University and collaborators have used a highly sensitive laser device to register infrasonic vibrations in the human body.

They discovered that the observed vibrations are connected with the cardiovascular system, which has its own proper movements occurring simultaneously with the work of the heart. Three types of infrasonic vibrations were registered. Waves of the first type are connected with the heartbeat, the second with the human respiratory rhythm, and the third, called Traube-Hering waves, with emotional states.

Bruce Tainio, a famous researcher and developer of Tainio Technology, found that a healthy body resonates at a frequency of 62-70 MHz, and when your frequency drops to 58 MHz, that is when disease starts.

Bacterias, viruses, and disease each have their own low frequency that influences our energy field. When someone has a low frequency they are more susceptible to diseases, just like a non-alkaline diet can not only make your body acidic but can lower your frequency. Disharmonic and imbalance in the body's energy field shows up long before it becomes a physical problem. You want to keep your energy field and vibration high all the time. New technology, like Biodynamic technology, can help you understand your frequency and your energy more.

This is where the likened frequency is matched and based upon what you are emitting and attracting to you. Everything that is attracted, even joy, is a likened match to your energy. Your energy field is affected by what you listen to, you ingest, you think and the emotions you are cultivating, we can also call it your quantum environment.

The way you think, your perspective on things, which depends on your emotional world, is reflected in your attitude and all thought processes. So, you end up attracting to you whatever you think about and the way you think about it and how that makes you feel emotionally. If it has a likened energy frequency match, it will attract. If it doesn't have a match, it will not attract.

For example, if you are constantly feeling the emotion of envy, you will continue creating scenarios in your life in which you can feel that emotion again and again. You will constantly be attracting the same emotional frequencies and putting yourself in situations in which you feel jealousy or envy. You can change that if you work on yourself and break the toxic emotional patterns by installing new healthy ones.

This is how it all works. When you raise your consciousness, you start attracting the same conscious match to you in everything you do. You begin to change your perspective, and so many matching frequencies start to show up in different ways.

Through experiments and focus groups, David Hawkin's developed the levels of consciousness. He makes the link between emotions, consciousness, and frequencies, and uses the frequency of energy to determine the level of consciousness. Here it is:

LEVELS OF CONSCIOUSNESS

Name of Level	Energetic "Frequency"	Associated Emotional State	View Of Life
Enlightenment	700 - 1000	Ineffable	Is
Peace	600	Bliss	Perfect
Joy	540	Serenity	Complete
Love	500	Reverence	Benign
Reason	400	Understanding	Meaningful
Acceptance	350	Forgiveness	Harmonious
Willingness	310	Optimism	Hopeful
Neutrality	250	Trust	Satisfactory
Courage	200	Affirmation	Feasible
Pride	175	Scorn	Demanding
Anger	150	Hate	Antagonistic
Desire	125	Craving	Disappointing
Fear	100	Anxiety	Frightening
Grief	75	Regret	Tragic
Apathy	50	Despair	Hopeless
Guilt	30	Blame	Evil
Shame	20	Humiliation	Miserable

Did you notice that Joy is in the top three of a higher consciousness? 540 Hz is the frequency of Joy vs. Guilt with 30 Hz. A higher conscious level can be achieved with joy, peace, enlightenment...

Everyone or everything that holds matter has the capacity to be attracted to everyone else or everything else, merely based upon where you are sitting within the frequency, or where the vibration matches. This is how you base the decisions you make on a daily basis unconsciously; according to what you are matching within a certain frequency, or what you are attracting in your vibrational field.

When you don't like what is going on in your life, you need to alter your vibration. This different vibration will then attract a different outcome.

The longer you stay at an energy frequency in your existence, the more you are able to attract back to you likened energy frequency... because it matches.

There are numerous ways that you can raise your energy or frequency as a human being, and the answer is a combination of many concepts, habits, thoughts, and practices that we will explore throughout this book. Anything that comes from Enlightenment, Peace, Joy, Love is of a higher frequency. Anything that comes from Fear, Guilt, Shame is from a low frequency.

You must change your frequency in order to change anything that comes or goes on in your life. If you want to make the joyful leap, you must raise your frequency. Learning how to create a new thought, a new attitude towards all thoughts will result in a far more expansive experience. You can eliminate limitations and suffering by seeing and feeling things differently. You can focus on joy and transform your life completely by raising your vibration and attracting what you really want.

ASK YOURSELF:

1. Which emotions am I feeling right now? Am I feeling more than one emotion at the same time or only one?
2. What is the frequency of those emotions?
3. What is that emotion responding to in the 5 Elements of Behavior?
4. What can I do today to raise my frequency through joy and happiness?
5. At the end of your day, how do you usually feel about things?
6. Are the answers to all of these questions affecting my energy and your frequency? How?
7. How am I and what is going on in my life?
8. How aware am I of my emotions?

PRINCIPLE 16

Elevate your Vibration.

HAPPINESS IS A PERSPECTIVE

Happiness mainly comes from our own attitude, rather than from external factors."

-Dalai Lama

How can we experience joy and happiness in our life?"

THIS IS THE question that most humans ask themselves when experiencing life on Earth. Naturally, we all want happiness; nobody really wants to suffer on this planet and experience a dreadful and dark life. No one wants to take part in a sorrowful moment, trauma, or a bad day. We are all meant to be happy and experience the joy of life; the challenge comes when we get entangled with unhealthy emotional patterns, and it seems like we cannot break free from them.

We continue feeding those emotions and therefore attracting situations in which we recreate those unhealthy emotions all over again. To be happy is to be an emotional bullfighter, in which you manage to not be in fear, affected, or victimized by the bull running towards you.

While the components of the emotions we feel are present in all individuals, the intensity and expression of these emotions differ from one person to another. There are also social factors like gender, culture, and epigenetics, that influence on why people may feel emotions differently despite similar situations.

Seeing things from another perspective influences our emotional world, and having a different perspective is like wearing glasses. When you wear sunglasses, for example, you see the world through the lens of the glasses, and sometimes the glasses can enhance the colors you are seeing.

To be joyful and happy requires courage, discipline, mindfulness, temperance, and being grounded. At the beginning of your journey towards happiness, you might feel discouraged at times, but after your "happy glasses" or "happy filter" is active, healthy, and strong, you won't stop finding reasons to be happy.

How each individual perceives and experiences life depends on their perspective. Someone's perspective is built through the years from information and emotional patterns we learn through our family, friends, society, cultural background, social media, the media, etc.

You can look at anything, even challenges or "problems", and if you run it through the "happy filter" or "happy glasses", you will find a new perspective and a reason to be happy about it. Believe me! You will find out that you are a new person when you get to the other side of challenges; you have learned something new, and you are now a better you.

LOOKING FOR THE GOOD IN EVERY SITUATION IS LIKE WEARING THE "HAPPY GLASSES"

There is unconditional happiness, and conditional happiness.

The difference between conditional and unconditional is that in conditional happiness you need to satisfy a condition to be happy which means you will often tell yourself that "I can be happy if" the "if" is the definition of conditional happiness, your happiness depends on something outside your present truth.

Unconditional happiness is all about being happy in the now no matter what is going on in your life. When you anchor the reasons for your happiness in an unconditional way, the source of your happiness will never vanish, and you will always find new reasons to be happy once you apply the "happy glasses".

The majority of people in the world are searching for conditional happiness. Our whole life, we think that happiness is from achievement or when all the right things happen to us. In reality, we are just creating rules and limits for ourselves, rules about when we can be happy.

IMAGINE YOUR FATE POSITIVELY

We should constantly be inspired by the idea of living and thriving with a happy life no matter the circumstances we are in. Always expecting the best outcome for our life. Happiness is just a perspective, and that you can wear the "happy glasses" for any circumstance in life, just try it!

ASK YOURSELF:

1. How am I feeling right now?
2. What emotions am I experiencing?
3. Which scenarios of my life can be optimized with the "happy filter"?
4. How can I continue to grow and expand if I choose happiness in the scenarios I am living in?
5. Am I in a healthy environment?
6. Am I in a toxic environment while surrounded by toxic people?
7. Is this challenge I am facing out of my control?
8. How am I growing with this challenge? What am I learning?
9. What can I do to experience happiness and joy while I navigate this challenge?

PRINCIPLE 17

Happiness is a perspective, wear "Happy Glasses".

PRINCIPLE 18

Focus on experiencing unconditional happiness.

JOY, HAPPINESS AND THE BLISS

The fact is always obvious much too late, but the most singular difference between happiness and joy is that happiness is a solid and joy a liquid."

– J.D. Salinger.

IF WE CONTINUE to explore the idea that happiness is a "filter", a "perspective", a tool that you can use in life to see through; Joy, on the other hand, is a force of nature that is born from within and not a filter or perspective. For example, a child, in most cases, brings joy to the parents. The satisfaction of helping people without expecting something in return can bring joy to someone's life. A good lover can bring so much joy to your life, and so on. Experiences, travels, pets, and even gardening. Joy is a source closer to peace and enlightenment. Happiness is more of a psychological reaction.

If you win the lottery you will find immediate exorbitant happiness, you will probably buy a new house, new car, go on a luxurious trip around the globe, and you will create many new happy memories. Now, after a few months of your new lifestyle, the happiness created by the lottery ticket will wear out, and you will go to your new normal levels of happiness. The reason for this is because happiness can be ephemerous while joy is longer lasting; the joy of your life could last forever. Happiness can be temporary; joy can be eternal.

We should aim to live a joyful life and allow happiness to filter our experiences.

JOY

> *I wake up every morning with a great desire to live joyfully."*
>
> – Anna Howard Shaw

Joy is a stronger, less common feeling than happiness. Witnessing or achieving selflessness to the point of personal sacrifice frequently triggers this emotion. Also feeling spiritually connected to a god or to people.

Joy is caused by spiritual experiences, caring for others, gratitude, thankfulness. The emotions are inward peace and contentment. It is longer lasting, based on inward circumstances.

Joy is that sudden burst of happiness. Joy is like the elevator in that building that takes you up to higher levels of experiencing life.

We can also find joy in the world through nature, relationships, friendships, social and political experiences. You can find joy in yourself, in your story, your life achievements, your self-realization, your actions, in the love and nurturing of your body.

HAPPINESS

Happiness: a state of well-being and contentment. The quality or state of being happy. Good fortune; pleasure; contentment. A feeling of contentment, satisfaction, and intense pleasure.

Caused by earthly experiences, material objects. Emotions are with outward expression of elation. Temporary, based on outward circumstances.

Happiness can be experienced from any good activity, food, or company. You can also activate happiness by wearing the "happy glasses".

THE BLISS

Bliss may be defined as a perfect state of joy and happiness, also defined as a natural direction you can take as a way to maximize your sense of joy, fulfillment, and purpose. Sometimes people equate bliss with being in a state of euphoria, but in reality, being blissful is the state you're in when you're doing what brings you a deep sense of joy and happiness at the same time. When you're in a blissful state, you're listening to the voice of your heart.

Joseph Campbell_was one of the pioneers in the discussion of bliss, suggesting that people "find their bliss." He said,

> *The way to find out what makes you the happiest is to focus on being mindful of your happiest moments, not simply excited, not just thrilled, but deeply happy."*

This requires paying attention to yourself and being mindful of the sensations in your body, and the thoughts fluttering around in your mind when you are actually joyful and happy. It also involves engaging in a bit of self-analysis.

If you engage in activities that make you happy, then you can move in the direction of your full potential or self-realization. These are markers or life-enhancing moments that you can keep track of in your journal. Most of us strive toward self-realization, intuitively knowing that it is the deepest place of satisfaction and bliss. Maslow identified peak experiences or life-changing moments that could result in an individual moving in the direction of bliss. He believed that people who are highly evolved, such as mystics, are those who've experienced these peak moments, which can result in bliss.

To achieve and maintain a state of bliss, it's important to be open-minded and to be a risk-taker, walking the road less traveled. Think about those who exude bliss and examine their lives to see what traits they possess. An example of someone who took a risk that paid off was the main character in the book "The Little Prince" by Antoine de Saint-Exupéry. The protagonist is a pilot stranded on a desert with a non-functioning airplane. A man who calls himself a prince appears from another planet.

He suggests that the pilot goes with him to the desert to find water. Initially, the pilot declines, thinking it's safer to stay with his aircraft. Against what he considers his best judgment, the pilot decides to accompany the prince in the search for water. Just about the time when the pilot thinks he made a wrong decision, both men come upon a well with water. Had the pilot not trusted the prince, or had he not taken the risk to venture on this new path, he would probably still be stuck in the desert with a broken-down plane. The moral of the story is that in order to find your bliss and make your joyful leaps, you need to be a risk-taker.

ASK YOURSELF:

1. Does what I ingest bring me joy?
2. Are my actions matching the levels of happiness and joy I am seeking?
3. When was the first time I remember feeling the bliss? Have I ever felt that before?
4. Which friends bring joy to my life?
5. Does my work bring me joy or happiness?
6. Does my family bring me joy?
7. How would a list of things that bring me joy vs. happiness look like?
8. When was the last time I was in a state of bliss?
9. What am I willing to risk in order to make the joyful leap?

PRINCIPLE 19

Take risks to ascend to a State of Bliss.

QUANTUM JOYFULNESS

You can conquer almost any fear if you will only make up your mind to do so. For remember, fear doesn't exist anywhere except in the mind."

— Dale Carnegie

To understand what "Quantum Joyfulness" is all about is important to understand that Quantum mechanics is the best theory we have for describing the world at a level of atoms and subatomic particles. It is really cool! In the future, we will all have quantum technology computers! They already exist, and I can't wait!

Perhaps the most renowned mystery of quantum mechanics is the fact that the outcome of a quantum experiment can change depending on whether or not we choose to measure some property of the particles involved, meaning it changes depending on the focus of the observer.

When this "observer effect" was first noticed by the early pioneers of quantum theory, they were deeply troubled. It seemed to undermine the basic assumption behind all science: that there is an objective world out there, irrespective of us. If the way the world behaves depends on how we look at it, what can "reality" really mean? This also means that the way we think of our own outcome can actually influence it.

Quantum Physics is described as the most powerful science conceived by human beings. It is really the most groundbreaking science we have until this moment because Quantum Physics can be applied to human behavior, emotions, and thoughts and how it shapes an individual's outcome or reality. A "Quantum Leap" describes a drastic quantum change within the behavior of an atom.

Fred Alan Wolf, in his award-winning book titled Taking the Quantum Leap, describes the term as,

> ...the explosive jump that a particle of matter undergoes in moving from one place to another... in a figurative sense, taking the quantum leap means taking a risk, going off into an uncharted territory with no guide to follow."

Taking the quantum leap is about skipping levels and just going for it, not focusing on the road but in the destination, the goal, the purpose, instead of wanting to be something, knowing that you are already that something. It is taking a drastic jump from point A to point Z without stopping in between. In order to do so, it is fundamental to take big risks, thinking beyond common sense, ignoring conventional approaches, trusting on your purpose and dreams, and really focusing on the end rather than means.

Quantum Physics affirms that we are the observers, the audience of a show with our name, and that we have the power to tell our story however we want and make it a joyful one.

"Quantum Joyfulness" is about knowing that you are already joyful as oppose to wanting to live a joyful life, like being your own observer observing a joyful life that is unbreakable—being able to drastically change your energy-conscious environment and living the bliss of life.

Harvard psychology professor Dan Gilbert talks about how happiness can be "synthesized" or created. Sir Thomas Brown wrote in 1642,

> I am the happiest man alive. I have that in me that can convert poverty to riches, adversity to prosperity. I am more invulnerable than Achilles; fortune hath not one place to hit me."

What is going on with this guy? Is he made out of iron? What's happening is that he deeply believes that he is happy! He truly believes he is everything he is saying about himself and an energetic match for him. That is what making the Joyful leap or creating synthetic happiness is about. Drastically changing your quantum environment to support your joyful life, the one you truly believe to possess.

"The Happy Filter" and "Quantum Joyfulness" work together. The happy filter helps you to deal with problems and solve them. While quantum joyfulness grounds your joy and happiness in the reality you are creating as your own observer and risk-taker. You're absolutely true!

ASK YOURSELF:

1. How committed to creating a constantly joyful reality and which risks am I willing to take?
2. How can I apply quantum joyfulness to my life and make joyful leaps every day?
3. How will I know I have made a joyful leap?
4. Am I the observer of my own reality, or is it someone or soothing else?

PRINCIPLE 20

Become the observer-creator of your own life and fill it with joy.

PART III

TRAUMAS, HEALING, AND TRANSFORMING

TRAUMAS

> *In Buddhism there is the idea of dispositions and imprints left by certain types of experiences, which is somewhat similar to the idea of the unconscious in Western psychology. For instance, a certain type of event may have occurred in an earlier part of your life which has left a very strong imprint on your mind which can remain hidden, and then later affect your behavior. So, there is this idea of something that can be unconscious imprints that one may not be consciously aware of."*
>
> – Dalai Lama

THE PATH TOWARDS happiness is not all peaches and cream; before you are ready to fully invite joy and happiness into your life, you have to do some house cleaning. It is important that you free yourself from what is holding you back in life before experiencing joy and living the life you've always dreamed of. You will need to do some digging inside of you at the events that might have left a strong imprint in your emotional patterns, or that you might have learned from your family or someone. Let me tell you a story.

1950. Selma was the only child born into a bourgeois class family in Louisiana. Her mother and father gave her everything she wanted. They raised her to become a good wife and mother, even though deep inside, she wanted to become a pianist. For a woman at that time, the arts were not necessarily the profession her parents wanted, or society would accept easily. Back then, women were just entering the workforce and getting their right to vote.

Selma married a young man and left her parent's home to live with her new husband, an engineer that was just returning from the war. It was her first love, and it was too late, after having three children and having a husband who was an alcoholic who was mismanaging their money with his addiction. She became so depressed and anxious about losing the lifestyle she always knew of that her frustration about finances, and an alcoholic husband grew more every day.

Her only emotional support was her mother, but after the bank took away one of the properties of Selma's husband, she was determined to take away her life and the life of her three children with her. She thought no children deserved to come to the world into a poor family. In a rage of anger, fear of being poor and feeling helpless, she got them all in the car and drove to the bridge of the town with the intention of driving the car off the bridge. Her plan failed, she just smashed the car against the concrete, but the imprint left in her three children of that experience became a huge one. The oldest one, Katheryn, got so rebellious against her mother from that moment on that she went to live with her grandmother who raised her.

Katheryn became a woman and had a child of her own, who she also abandoned when he was about the same age of her traumatic event, and sent the newborn boy to live with his grandmother, Selma. Do you see the pattern? The son of Katheryn, Jason, also had a child who he also passed on that same unhealthy pattern to.

This is the reality for so many people; the way they behave sometimes is just learned behavior and traumas passed on for many generations. We need to step back, look at our behavior, bringing awareness and mindfulness to it, and make sure that it represents who we really are.

There are two types of traumatic experiences, "Organic Traumas", that have more to do with genetics, what your family or what society taught you, and imprints and patterns like the one in Selma's story, and we have on the second experience (PTSD), Post Traumatic Stress Disorder.

WHAT IS POST TRAUMATIC STRESS DISORDER?

Some people have the misfortune of witnessing or being the victims of traumatic events such as emotional or physical abuse, accidents, civil unrest, war, and natural disasters.

As you can imagine, such events can inflict profound emotional wounds that don't always heal fully with time.

Post-traumatic stress disorder is a condition that occurs in apparently healthy individuals who've been exposed to extreme stressors such as car accidents, sexual assault, war, unexpected deaths, etc. In general, people with PTSD experience flashbacks, hypervigilance, panic attacks, and insomnia. On top of that, many of them are at risk of developing depression or anxiety.

But not all people who survive a traumatic event end up struggling with PTSD. Even if your immediate response to a traumatic event is extreme, it's not a sign of mental illness. In fact, it's perfectly normal to have an intense reaction to a potentially traumatic event. The problem occurs when we can't get past the painful memories that might follow, and we just fall in a spiral.

PTSD is an anxiety disorder characterized by three broad categories of problems: involuntary recurrent memories of past trauma, avoidance of trauma-associated stimuli, and persistent hyperactivity, and hypervigilance. If you feel you are experiencing PTSD, you should seek professional help.

People who are dealing with PTSD can experience a wide array of physiological and psychological symptoms, including:

- Flashbacks
- Recurrent memories of past traumatic experiences
- Insomnia, nightmares, and night terrors
- Memory gaps
- Muscle tension
- Restlessness and vigilance
- Guilt and sadness
- Lack of focus
- Outbursts of anger
- Self-destructive behaviors
- Crushing feeling of loneliness and isolation
- Agoraphobia
- An overall grim perspective on the future

If you experience PTSD symptoms for more than a few weeks, make sure to consult a licensed mental health professional. Also, keep in mind that sometimes symptoms do not manifest until six months or more after the traumatic event.

The transmission of trauma may be particular to a given family suffering a loss, such as the death of an infant, or it can be a shared response to societal trauma.

Traumas are often passed on through unconscious cues or affective messages that flow between adult and child. Sometimes anxiety falls from one generation to the next through stories told and belief systems.

YOU CAN HEAL YOUR ANCESTORS TRAUMAS IN YOURSELF AND BE FREE

Transgenerational transmissions take on life in our dreams, in acting out, in "life lessons" given in turns of phrase and taught to us by our family. Discovering transmission means coming to know and tell a larger narrative, one from the preceding generation. It requires close listening to the stories of our parents and grandparents, with special attention to the social and historical milieu in which they lived, especially its military, economic, and political turmoil. How do we carry secret stories from before our lifetimes?

The emotional ties between children and ancestors are essential to the development of our values. These bonds often determine the answers to questions such as: "Who am I?" "Who am I to my family?" "Who can 'we' trust" and who are our enemies?", "What ties me to my family?" And, most importantly, "of these ties, which do I reject, and which do I keep?"

How does one discharge this mission? It is a precarious terrain of finding one's way through a web of familial loyalties to which one has been intensely faithful. The working through of transmission entails a painful, seemingly unbearable, process of separation. It can become an identity crisis, the breaking of an emotional chain. As Fromm puts it,

"something life defining and deeply intimate is over."

86

The child speaks about what their parent could not. He or she recognizes how their own experience has been authored, how one has been authorized if unconsciously, to carry their parents' injury into the future. In rising above the remnants of one's ancestors' trauma, one helps to heal future generations.

> *So, when you can't explain what is causing certain behaviors or problems, the tendency is to always attribute it to the unconscious. It's a bit like you've lost something, and you decide that the object is in this room."*
>
> – Dalai Lama

ASK YOURSELF:

1. Do you feel overwhelmed?
2. Do you have flashbacks?
3. Do you often "space out"?
4. Do you overreact or respond inappropriately?
5. Do you feel ashamed about something?
6. Do you have continued thoughts or memories related to the event?
7. Do you have recurring dreams about the event?
8. Do you have flashbacks of the trauma?
9. Do you have a difficult time when anything triggers a memory of the event?
10. Do you try to avoid thinking about the trauma or avoid memories of it?
11. Do you try to avoid people, places, conversations, objects, or activities that are associated with the trauma?
12. Do you have a difficult time remembering details of the trauma?
13. Do you have negative beliefs about yourself, such as "I am bad" or "people are untrustworthy"?
14. Do you blame yourself for the trauma?
15. Are you in a continued state of feeling guilt, shame, anger, fear, or horror?
16. Do you have less interest in activities you used to enjoy?
17. Do you find it difficult to experience love, joy, happiness, satisfaction?

18. Do you have difficulty sleeping?
19. Do you have difficulty concentrating?
20. Do you have anger outbursts?
21. Are you in a constant state of worrying about something bad happening?
22. Do you behave recklessly or engage in self-destructive behavior?
23. How will I know I have identified my traumas?
24. How will I know I have healed my traumas?

PRINCIPLE 21

Face your Traumas.

EMOTIONAL PATTERNS

"Change happens in the boiler room of our emotions, so find out how to light their fires."

— Jeff Dewar

E MOTIONAL-BEHAVIORAL PATTERNS ARE habitual and defensive reactions to past events that are projected in the field of the present time so that all that is happening is effectively repetitive and limiting. Many family generations have passed many emotional patterns; some patterns are even deep inside our DNA.

Besides the family, there are many factors contributing to someone developing unhealthy emotional patterns, like cultural background, social groups, and life-changing events.

Emotional-behavioral patterns remind us of our mechanical nature of learning and repeating. Because when you start a pattern, there is an irresistible compulsion to see it through. It is impossible not to! Like riding a train, you buy your ticket, and the moment the train leaves the station, the outcome is assured. You enter the initiatory event of a negative emotional-behavioral pattern, and the rest inevitably follows. You seem to be completely helpless.

The way someone can step out of unhealthy emotional-behavioral patterns is through awareness. By becoming aware of how you react, from the very first interaction to the last, you become aware of the protective predictability of your unconscious patterning.

Once you have identified some of your emotional patterns, you can intersect them and transform them into fuel for your life. Here are some examples of how you can break unhealthy patterns:

89

ASK YOURSELF:

1. Which emotions am I feeling right now?
2. Which emotions are my "go-to" emotions?
3. Why? When did I start feeling that way?
4. How old was I? What was going on in my life at the time?
5. Did someone make me feel that way, or I chose to feel that way?
6. Who was next to me the very first time I felt that way?
7. How do I feel about that person?
8. How does that person make me feel now?
9. When else did I feel that way? (Mention each time and write it on a timeline)
10. What kind of actions have I taken since I am feeling these emotions?
11. How do those actions make me feel now?
12. What can I do to transform those actions?
13. How can I create new emotional patterns that invite happiness and joy into my life?
14. How will I know I am cultivating new positive emotional patterns?

PRINCIPLE 22

Develop positive emotional Patterns.

THE SHADOW

> *The shadow is a moral problem that challenges the whole ego-personality, for no one can become conscious of the shadow without considerable moral effort. To become conscious of it involves recognizing the dark aspects of the personality as present and real. This act is the essential condition for any kind of self-knowledge."*
>
> – Carl Jung, *Aion* (1951)

THE "SHADOW" IS a concept first coined by Swiss psychiatrist Carl Jung that describes those aspects of the personality that we choose to reject and repress. For one reason or another, we all have parts of ourselves that we don't like, or that we think society won't like, so we push those parts down into our unconscious psyches. It is this collection of repressed aspects of our identity that Jung referred to as our shadow.

If you're one of those people who generally love who they are, you might be wondering whether this is true in you. "I don't reject myself," you might be thinking. "I love everything about me."

However, the problem is that you're not necessarily aware of those parts of your personality that you reject.

According to Jung's theory, we distance ourselves psychologically from those behaviors, emotions, and thoughts that we find dangerous.

Rather than confront something that we don't like, our mind pretends it does not exist. Aggressive impulses, taboo mental images, shameful experiences, immoral urges, fears, irrational wishes, unacceptable sexual desires, these are a few examples of shadow aspects, things people contain but do not admit to themselves that they contain.

Here are a few examples of common shadow behaviors:

1. **A tendency to harshly judge others, especially if that judgment comes on an impulse.** You may have caught yourself doing this once or twice when you pointed out to a friend how "ridiculous" someone else's outfit looked. Deep down, you would hate to be singled out this way, so doing it to another reassures you that you're smart enough not to take the same risks as the other person.

2. **Pointing out one's own insecurities as flaws in another.** The internet is notorious for hosting this. Scan any comments section, and you'll find an abundance of trolls calling the author and other commenters "stupid," "moron," "idiot," "untalented," "brainwashed," and so on. Ironically, internet trolls are some of the most insecure people of all.

3. **A quick temper with people in subordinate positions of power.** People are quick to cop an attitude with people who don't have the power to fight back. Exercising power over another is the shadow's way of compensating for one's own feelings of helplessness in the face of greater force.

4. **Frequently playing the "victim" of every situation.** Rather than admit wrongdoing, people go to amazing lengths to paint themselves as the poor, innocent bystander who never has to take responsibility.

5. **A willingness to step on others to achieve one's own ends.** People often celebrate their own greatness without acknowledging times that they may have cheated others to get to their success. You can see this happen on the micro-level as people vie for position in checkout lines and cut each other off in traffic. On the macro level, corporations rig policy in their favor to gain tax cuts at the expense of the lower classes.

6. **Unacknowledged biases and prejudices.** People form assumptions about others based on their appearance all the time; in fact, it's a pretty natural (and often useful, e.g., noticing signs of a dangerous person) thing to do. However, we can easily take this too far, veering into toxic prejudice. But with so much social pressure to eradicate prejudice, people often find it easier to "pretend" that they're not racist/homophobic/xenophobic/sexist,

etc., than to do the deep work it would take to override or offset particularly destructive stereotypes they may be harboring.

7. **A messiah complex.** Some people think they're so "enlightened" that they can do no wrong. They construe everything they do as an effort to "save" others, to help them "see the light," so to speak. This is actually an example of spiritual bypassing, yet another manifestation of the shadow.

Projection, seeing Our Darkness in Others. Seeing the shadow within ourselves is extremely difficult, so it's rarely done, but we're really good at seeing undesirable shadow traits in others. Truth be told, we revel in it. We love calling out unsightly qualities in others. In fact, the entire celebrity gossip industry is built on this fundamental human tendency.

Seeing in others what we won't admit also lies within is what Jung calls "projection." Although our conscious minds are avoiding our own flaws, they still want to deal with them on a deeper level, so we magnify those flaws in others. First, we reject, then we project.

"Shadow work", then, is the process of making the unconscious conscious. In doing so, we gain awareness of our unconscious impulses and can then choose whether and how to act on them. We begin this process when we take a step back from our normal patterns of behavior and observe what is happening within us. Meditation is a great way to develop this ability to step back from ourselves, with the goal being to gain the ability to do this as we go about our daily lives.

The next step is to question. When we observe ourselves reacting to psychological triggers or events that prompt an instant and uncontrolled reaction from us, we must learn to pause and ask ourselves, "Why am I reacting this way?" This teaches us to backtrack through our emotions to our memories, which hold the origins of our emotional programming.

Identifying triggers can be a difficult process due to our natural desire to avoid acknowledging the shadow. Our tendency is to justify our actions after the fact when really the best thing we can do is avoid acting reactively or unconsciously in the first place. Cultivating an awareness of the shadow is the first step to identifying our triggers, but before we can do that, we must first overcome our instinctive fear of our shadows.

DEALING WITH THE ANGER FOR TRAUMAS OR SHADOW

If you feel your own shadow coming your way, practice mindfulness and disassociate from the emotion or thought coming with it. Intersect it using the "Five Elements of Behavior", and from that moment in the present time, change that emotion or thought for one that represents your happiness.

If you are dealing with a lot of anger, a good exercise you can practice releasing that anger is throwing rocks at a lake, river, or ocean. Boxing is a good way of releasing anger, working out. Releasing anger, frustration, and sadness is part of healing and letting go. Just bring mindfulness and awareness, so you release it and move on as opposed to staying in that emotion. Always think about the emotion you want rather to feel. Is it joy? Then go for it!

You can also write a letter with all the reasons for your anger towards family, friends, or anyone who left a traumatic imprint in you. It can be about your own shadow, writing down all the reasons, forgiving them, or forgiving yourself and letting it go. In the end, burn it in a safe way, and be free.

ASK YOURSELF:

1. Is there anything I am trigged by easily?
2. Why do I react like that whenever I hear about it?
3. When was the first time I remember reacting like that?
4. Was that thought originally integrated into my awareness by a family member, friend, or another person?
5. Am I holding onto beliefs or ideas that don't serve my happiness and joy?
6. How will I know I am no longer holding unconscious ideas that don't serve me anymore?

PRINCIPLE 23

Overcome your shadow.

FORGIVENESS

"Forgiveness does not change the past, but it does enlarge the future."

– Paul Boose

ONE OF THE first steps in learning how to forgive yourself is to focus on your emotions. Before you can move forward, you need to acknowledge and process your emotions. Give yourself permission to recognize and accept the feelings that have been triggered in you and welcome them.

Acknowledge the mistakes out loud, write it down in a list. If you make a mistake and continue to struggle with letting it go, acknowledge out loud what you learned from the mistake.

When you give a voice to the thoughts in your head and the emotions in your heart, you may free yourself from some of the burdens. You also imprint in your mind what you learned from your actions and consequences.

Think of each "mistake" as a learning experience that holds the key to moving forward faster and more consistently in the future. Reminding ourselves that we did the best we could with the tools and knowledge we had at the time, will help us forgive ourselves and move forward.

If you make a mistake but have a hard time putting it out of your mind, visualize your thoughts and feelings about the mistake going into a container, such as a mason jar or box. Ask yourself what you have learned from it, you can also write it down in a piece of paper that you burn down as a promise to yourself through forgiveness that such an event won't ever be holding you back in life.

Have a conversation with your inner critic, and of course, journaling can help you understand your inner critic and develop self-compassion. One thing you can do is write out a "conversation" between you and your inner critic. This can help you identify thought patterns that are sabotaging your ability to forgive yourself.

You can also use journaling time to make a list of the qualities you like about yourself. This can help boost your self-confidence when you're feeling down about a mistake you made.

Notice when you are being self-critical. We are our own worst critics, right?

Quiet the negative messages of your inner critic. Sometimes it can be difficult to recognize the thoughts that are getting in the way of forgiveness. If you're struggling to sort out your inner critic, Pickell suggests this exercise:

On one side of a piece of paper, write down what your inner critic says (which tends to be critical and irrational).

On the other side of the paper, write a self-compassionate and rational response for each thing you wrote on the other side of the paper. Get clear about what you want.

ASK YOURSELF:

1. Do I feel any emotion from past mistakes I made that I need to transform and let go by forgiving myself?
2. Which person in my life have I not forgiven?
3. What happened?
4. How they made me feel?
5. How do I feel now about it?
6. Why keep carrying this event with me?
7. How is this event holding me back from my new expansion?
8. How can I let go and transform this event in a way that invites Happiness and Joy into my life?
9. How will I know I have forgiven myself?

10. How will I know that I have forgiven other people that harmed me in the past?
11. How will that freedom look like?
12. How will that affect my happiness?

PRINCIPLE 24

Forgive yourself and others.

LET GO OF THE PAST

You can't feed today's hunger with yesterday's meal."

– TJ Milam

F IT IS in the past, let it go. Only invite and let in what is happening right now, what is happening today, at this very moment. Sometimes we spend years carrying over the memory of a dream job, a lover, a friend, an experience. Let it go... Just like you would forget about some happy moments of yesterday.

Create a positive mantra to counter the painful thoughts. How you talk to yourself can either move you forward or keep you stuck. Often, having a mantra that you tell yourself in times of emotional pain can help you reframe your thoughts, and let go.

For example, says clinical psychologist Carla Manly, Ph.D., instead of getting stuck in, "I can't believe this happened to me!" try a positive mantra such as, "I am fortunate to be able to find a new path in life, one that is good for me."

Create physical distance. It's not uncommon to hear someone say that you should distance yourself from the person or situation that is causing you to be upset, especially after COVID-19.

According to clinical psychologist Ramani Durvasula, Ph.D., that's not such a bad idea. "Creating physical or psychological distance between ourselves and the person or situation can help with letting go for the simple reason that we are not having to think about it, process it, or be reminded of it as much," she explains.

Do your own work, focusing on yourself is important. You have to make the choice to address the hurt that you've experienced. When you think about a person who caused you pain, bring yourself back to the present. Then, focus on something that you're grateful for. You can also write the experience, emotions, and details down on a paper and burn it as a ritual of letting go.

Practice mindfulness and be gentle with yourself. If your first response to not being able to let go of a painful situation is to criticize yourself, it's time to show yourself some kindness and compassion.

We should be treating ourselves like we would treat a friend, offering ourselves self-compassion, and avoiding comparisons between our journey and those of others.

Hurt is inevitable, and we may not be able to able to avoid pain; however, we can choose to treat ourselves kindly and lovingly when it comes, and letting it go without sitting on it—just observing it—knowing the lesson that was there for us to grow. Then we can choose the emotion we would rather feel and go for it.

Allow the negative emotions to flow. If you're fear of feeling negative emotions is causing you to avoid them, don't worry, you're not alone. In fact, many times, people are afraid of feelings such as grief, anger, disappointment, or sadness.

Rather than feeling them, people just try to shut them out, which can disrupt the process of letting go, and that is not what ultimate joy and happiness are about. Let them go... Cry if you have to, let the emotions flow. These negative emotions most flow out of you before you can look at them as a learning and growth experience... It may require mental health intervention, but fighting them or ignoring them can leave you stuck.

Accept that the other person may not apologize. Waiting for an apology from the person who hurt you will slow down the process of letting go, forgive them first... If you're experiencing hurt and pain, it's important you take care of your own healing, which may mean accepting that the person who hurt you isn't going to apologize, but their actions should not determine your own happiness. You are you, and only responsible for yourself, the best you can do is forgive them and move on towards your joy.

Engage in self-care; when we are hurting, it often feels like there is nothing but hurt. Practicing self-care can look like setting boundaries, saying no, doing the things that bring us joy and comfort, and listening to our own needs first.

Surround yourself with people who fill you up. This simple yet powerful tip can help carry you through a lot of pain. We can't do life alone, and we can't expect ourselves to get through our hurts alone, friends can also help us to let go of things. Allowing ourselves to lean on loved ones and their support is such a wonderful way of not only limiting isolation but of reminding us of the good that is in our lives.

When you're dealing with painful feelings or a situation that hurt you, it's important to give yourself permission to talk about it.

Sometimes people can't let go because they feel they aren't allowed to talk about it, and therefore they can't let go of things. This may be because the people around them no longer want to hear about it, or the person is embarrassed or ashamed to keep talking about it.

But talking it out is important. That's why finding a friend or therapist who is patient and accepting as well as willing to be your sounding board is imperative to let go if you need the support.

Forgiveness is vital to the healing process because it allows you to let go of anger, guilt, shame, sadness, or any other feeling you may be experiencing and move on. Seek professional help if you're struggling to let go of a painful experience, you may benefit from talking to a professional. Sometimes it's difficult to implement these tips on your own; self-help is a beautiful thing, but sometimes you need an experienced professional to help guide you through the process.

ASK YOURSELF:

1. What kind of memory or person am I bringing from my past that is holding me back?
2. How is this memory or person continuing to nourish a toxic emotional pattern I might have?
3. What void do I think they are filling?
4. Why does that void exist in the first place?
5. How can I fill that void with self-love, happiness, and joyful memories?
6. How will I know that I have let go of a memory holding me back?
7. How will that look like?

PRINCIPLE 25

Let go of the Past.

INDEPENDENCE

" *The Highest Happiness is when one reaches a state of liberation.*"

– DL

HAPPINESS THAT DEPENDS on something external of your mind and body is unsustainable. Personal independence boosts your confidence, and it grounds you with your authentic self, truth, dreams, and your very own joy.

Independent people naturally tend to be a little more confident in handling issues affecting their lives. This is mainly because they are more prepared to take action and do things without having to wait for support or permission from someone else. Being independent, therefore, means that you will be more likely to try out new things that you want rather than what or how you are expected to. This also means that you will have more experience than a less independent individual. This will, in time, build up more confidence in you with the knowledge that you can do things on your own. For entrepreneurs, this confidence opens your mind to taking bigger risks and unbeaten paths that eventually return bigger rewards.

Less independent individuals tend to rely so much on others. This may be because they do not want to have to make choices for themselves, or they feel too shy to go through challenges in their life without somebody by their side. This character makes you appear overly needy. Being a little more independent will be much appreciated by people, and they will be willing to come to you for help. Being needed or relied upon is what many crave for, this will add some self-value on and understanding of your value in your community or environment.

Emotional independence reduces stress and promotes happiness. Being emotionally independent means that you can make the most of your personal decisions and go through challenging life situations without necessarily dragging other people into it. More emotional independence can also mean less suffering and disappointment since you do not depend on others to meet your emotional needs. It is, however, good to understand that social support is necessary, but you can still get it without necessarily being emotionally dependent on that social structure.

Financial independence means freedom and a sense of accomplishment!

When it comes to personal independence, there is no satisfaction comparable to the ability to pay your own bills. Being able to pay your way through life reduces dependence on your parents, friends, sugar daddy, spouse, or whichever person you used to lean on. Financial independence means that you control your income and expenditure, and you are not answerable to anybody unless it is the IRS or Tax Bureau. The more that you learn to become financially independent, the less stress you may have in your life as you are more in control of your financial outcome.

Being independent makes decision-making an easy task; this is because you have proven to yourself that you are the only person who will be really affected by your decisions. On the other hand, being dependent on other people for emotional or financial support makes it difficult to make clear and appropriate decisions; this is because you will always have to stop to think about how the other person will be affected, and how they will react to your decisions. Whereas it is a good idea to consider other people while making decisions, being scared to make choices in fear of upsetting others can greatly hold you back.

The idea of setting independence as a goal can greatly boost multiple aspects of your life. Emotional independence, for example, improves your personal relations with friends, family, workmates, and other people you interact with. You become more in control of your emotions, such as anger, over-excitement, anxiety, mood swings, and so on. Having a free and independent mind gives you the freedom to explore your skills and talents and will ultimately bring out the best in you.

Broader horizons, to be more independent, means being prepared and free to meet new people and try new things. This, in turn, means that you will develop a broader sense of the world and be open to people and new opportunities, which leads to more knowledge understanding of the world and yourself. It is in these deeper horizons that lie opportunities for success and adventure. Less independent individuals are less likely to have such opportunities. This is, in fact, what sets successful entrepreneurs apart from the rest.

Independence can help increase your self-value and self-esteem, more so if becoming independent is one of your goals. The achievement of financial, emotional, social, career, and personal independence gives you a sense of accomplishment that eventually changes how you rate yourself and how others view you. The increased self-worth that comes with this independence is a great booster to your self-esteem, personal success, and happiness.

Below is an amazing quote about being independent by Friedrich Nietzsche. I hope you enjoy his quote as much as I did,

> *It is the business of the very few to be independent; it is a privilege of the strong. And whoever attempts it, even with the best right, but without being obliged to do so, proves that he is probably not only strong, but also daring beyond measure. He enters into a labyrinth, he multiplies a thousand-fold the dangers which life in itself already brings with it; not the least of which is that no one can see how and where he loses his way, becomes isolated, and is torn piecemeal by some minotaur of conscience. Supposing such a one comes to grief, it is so far from the comprehension of men that they neither feel it, nor sympathize with it. And he cannot any longer go back! He cannot even go back again to the sympathy of men!"*

ASK YOURSELF:

1. Do I depend on someone financially or emotionally?
2. Who Is that person?
3. When was the first time I felt emotionally or financially dependent?
4. How can I become more independent in my daily life?
5. How will I know I am completely independent?

PRINCIPLE 26

Be happily independent.

HAPPINESS AND THE EGO

BASING YOUR HAPPINESS in what boost your ego won't last forever, and at one point, it will all collapse. Basing happiness on the idea of success, or being "pretty", young, rich, etc. Won't work!

Capitalism teaches us that having a big house, and the expensive car and the "hot" or "perfect" significant other is the meaning of happiness. Our society believes that material things or social status are the sources of happiness.

Narcissism, every single one of us, has a touch of narcissism in our being. How do I know this? Because it's evident in the way, we navigate our lives, regardless of who we are as people. In other words, our entire outlook on life is through the lens of our own personal experience and filtered with our biases, grudges, and to some people even social media.

Just think about the last moment in your life where something unfortunate happened to you. Maybe it was losing a job or a loved one, getting into a car accident, a breakup/divorce, or something else of equal impact. Our immediate thought is, "WHAT DID I DO TO DESERVE THIS?". This forms the slippery slope that many of us will refer to as "narcissism" following this read. This thought comes entirely from a place of 'there must have been something I did to deserve this because otherwise, it wouldn't have happened."

THE EGO

The demand for more, be it money, success, happiness, even love comes from that part of the mind that is the ego. Most people think of the ego as the behavioral trait of self-importance or overconfidence, and while it is to a degree, there is much more to the ego than that.

The ego is the part of our psychological make up that, no matter what we give it, is never happy. Imagine the ego as a child that has so many toys to play with and sweets to eat yet still continues to throw tantrums and wants more.

When you give the ego what it wants, it's only satisfied for a fraction of time, before it starts to want more again. You can never destroy the ego; it lives within all of us, even the most enlightened beings. However, you can learn to play the ego as its own game by tapping into a power far greater, actions from love and your heart, and simply ignoring the ego.

It's only the ego that believes, for example, that you need more money in order to be happy, or more "cool" friends to feel a sense of belonging, or a new shirt, a new expensive car, all the followers on social media, etc. The heart wants nothing material, just love, peace, joy.

After struggling for a few years in Los Angeles while I was attending film school, in 2015, I started my own video production company. It was my dream to do so, and I was beyond happy about finally being my own boss. Things started taking form really fast, and clients started referring me to other clients helping my business to grow. I was able to drive my dream car, wear that expensive clothing I wanted, and to buy me experiences that were bringing me happy moments. But after a few years of really making substantial income, my company suddenly dropped its hyperactive clientele. In the beginning, I started feeling fear, frustration, I was looking at my bills coming, and I started saying "no" to party invites and other social life that required money, and something interesting happened for the first time in my life: I lost part of my confidence.

I realized that all that purpose, love, happiness, and freedom that ignited the intention of starting my own company wasn't around anymore, and all that was left was my ego pissed off at the current financial situation of my company.

I thought wrongly that being successful was being financially thriving. I was so comfortable with my lifestyle, depending on certain levels of commodities that I was totally conditioned by it. My happiness was also depending on experiences that I needed money for, and that I couldn't afford anymore.

I became sad and even depressed for the second time in my life, and I couldn't even understand it because it wasn't about me being a material person but about me over-relying on money for my happiness. That, folks, is conditional happiness.

There's nothing wrong with money; money is just something for us to exchange value. A value that can also help you experience joy. The issue is when the bliss depends on money, then you are not free anymore.

I was a bit dramatic, and it seems funny now, but I even had suicidal thoughts because I truly felt alone and that there was no hope for my financial situation at that time. I only wanted to get my company back on track, but I was looping in this low frequency of lack, in fear, not knowing how I was going to pay my rent, my bills, the bills of the company, and without any other financial support or trust fund to rely upon.

But I realized one night that I could truly be joyful without depending on money to enjoy my happy experiences and places again. I realized that my fun and ideas had a bigger value than money and that my confidence didn't need money to exist, because It existed before on its own. I just needed to remember that again.

I remembered practicing mindfulness again, and just taking in the present moment with the beauty and the joy that was in front of me. That day I promised myself that I would never let my ego or any old wrong ideas of success be responsible for my confidence and happiness. The minute I had the breakthrough moment, the minute the phone of my company started ringing again. It was about making that emotional leap and letting my happiness break free and transcending while making my joyful leap.

The ego is not completely bad; in a way, we need the ego to get a sense of identity, goals, voice, and ambitions. People who say that you need to get rid of your ego, actually say that from their ego. The ego serves a purpose in our lives, just like experiencing sadness, but that doesn't mean we need to go through life feeding the ego or feeding our sadness. Because the ego will never be satisfied or happy if you listen to your ego, it will make you feel incomplete when that is not true.

I reconnected again from my heart to the mission and vision of my company and myself. I immediately knew what to do to get more new clients, and things got back to normal in less than a month, but it wasn't about the money anymore. I was able to experience life on a new level in which my ego wasn't having any control over my happiness. In which my joy was active again, free, present, and not depending on money or anything.

Each of these scenarios happens all the time, but we have just as frequent opportunities to act in a way that benefits our happiness and the personal fulfillment that is having independence. Being independent from the voice of your ego. Never let your ego control your life. Your ego will create vicious cycles of self-perception that is impractical and self-destructive. It is our job to humble ourselves with gratitude from our hearts.

ASK YOURSELF:

1. Which emotions am I feeling?
2. Are those emotions generated because I am taking advantage of an idea, someone, or abusing my power?
3. Is my happiness causing someone else to suffer?
4. How can I stop that from happening and transform it into happiness and joy?
5. Are my dreams feeding my joy or my ego?
6. Is my confidence depending on my ego?
7. Is my happiness depending on my ego?
8. Is my ego getting in my way of succeeding?
9. Is my ego getting in the way of new learnings or opportunities?
10. When was the last time I acted from my ego?

11. How have I changed since?
12. How can I prevent myself from taking actions from my ego?
13. How will I know my life is not run by my ego?

PRINCIPLE 27

Never let your happiness depend on your ego or boost your ego.

PRINCIPLE 28

Ignore your ego until it fades in the distance.

YOU ARE UNIQUE

WATER YOUR OWN grass. When we focus on other people, we lose time that we could otherwise invest in ourselves. We don't grow green grass by focusing on our neighbor's garden; we do it nurturing our own. So, instead of wasting time comparing your path to someone else's, spend it investing, creating, and caring for your own.

Accept where you are! You can't change something you don't acknowledge. So, instead of resisting or fighting where you are, come to peace with it. Say yes to every part of your life, and from that place, make decisions that will move you in the right direction.

Love your past and your story even more if life might have been messy and bumpy. It might have been colored by mistakes, anxiety, and fear. All those things were catalysts to help you become a better, wiser and more courageous version of yourself. So, embrace your story and how much you've grown from it. Be proud of what you've done and for wanting to create a better life for yourself.

Do a social media detox every other day. We're constantly bombarded with people who live #blessed lives on Instagram, Twitter, and Facebook. What we don't consider is that we often compare our own worst moments with someone else's highlight. Without mention that some of those social media #blessed types are just pretending and totally acting from their ego.

Social media can be a great source of inspiration, communication, and marketing. But, if it triggers inadequacy, self-doubt, and frustration, then

111

choose to do a detox. Make sure you control social media and not the other way around.

Know that this isn't the end of the movie. If you're not happy where you are today, remember that this is just a snapshot of your life. Where you are today doesn't say anything about where you'll be in one or three years from now, or who you even are. What matters isn't where you are. What matters is your mindset, attitude, what is in your heart, your values, your ideas, and where you're going.

Be grateful for what you have. Oprah said,

> *Be thankful for what you have; you'll end up having more. If you concentrate on what you don't have, you will never, ever have enough."*

Whenever you find yourself looking at what other people have, remind yourself of what you're grateful for. For me, that means appreciating my family, my wonderful friends, the things I create from my heart, the opportunities I can reach to or create, and the all experiences I have lived so far. The good and the not so good.

Realize that you're not perfect. There will always be someone who's richer, smarter, and more "attractive" than you. Everything is also a perspective, and that is the beauty of all of us being different. But if you feel unhappy with less, you will also feel unhappy with more. No one is perfect. Trying to be perfect is not the solution. So, instead of getting down on yourself for your flaws, quirks, and imperfections, accept them fully. Free yourself by embracing the fact that you're perfectly imperfect.

Be your own ally mean that the voice inside your head (your ego) can tell you all kinds of crap. Instead of joining in when the mean voice of comparison pops up, choose to be on your side. Relieve, soothe, and comfort yourself. Give yourself regular talks, and if you wouldn't say it to a friend, don't say it to yourself.

Turn comparison into inspiration as we tend to compare our behind-the-scenes with someone else's big moment. We tend to focus on their success, not on the thousands of hours they've spent preparing and working for their achievements. Instead of letting other people's triumphs be a time to get down on yourself, let it be a door opener to possibilities and celebrate their hard work. Let it be an inspiration for what you can be, do, and have in life.

Stop "shoulding" yourself. Comparison often leads to us "shoulding" all over ourselves. We say things such as, "I SHOULD have this by now" or "I SHOULD have come further." But statements like that just keep us focused on what we're lacking.

Instead of using "should" when expressing commitments, use "want", and to make the quantum leap say "have", and notice how your inner dialogue shifts.

If you need to compare yourself with someone, compare yourself with you. What can you do to improve your life quality? How can you be a better and more loving person? How can you be nicer to yourself than you were yesterday? You are the only person you can compare yourself with.

If the story you're telling yourself isn't one of empowerment, strength, and optimism, then tell a better story. Instead of telling yourself, you're not competent enough to do the work you want to do, tell yourself you're brave enough to try something new. Instead of blaming yourself for mistakes in the past, remind yourself that you did the best you could and that you've learned from it.

ASK YOURSELF:

1. Am I comparing myself with someone?
2. How?
3. What does that person possess that I don't?
4. How can I flag my truth and be proud of who I am without comparing myself?
5. How will that bring happiness and joy into my life?
6. How will I know I am not comparing myself with other people?

PRINCIPLE 29

Embrace every aspect of your truth.

PRINCIPLE 30

Only compare yourself to yourself.

LET GO OF TOXIC PEOPLE IN YOUR LIFE

> *People who suck positive energy from us disrupt our bodies' balance and harmony at the cellular level, weakening the immune system and leaving us susceptible to illness,"*
> — Florence Comite, M.D.

WE ARE GOING to discuss how to recognize toxic people and navigate the often difficult and emotional process of removing these toxic people from your life.

Because in a very real way, your future depends on it. "Toxic" gets overused a lot these days, so let's be clear about what we mean.

Some people in life are kind of a drag, annoying, difficult, energetic vampires, demanding, or otherwise unpleasant. These people are not "toxic" in the strict sense of the term. They're just generally undesirable. With this admittedly large group of people, you might want to create a little distance, but you won't have the same urgency to cut them out of your life.

Toxicity really exists on a spectrum. On one end, there's a friend that only drags you into his or her mess and doesn't even respect some boundaries. On the other end, there's your ex-girlfriend or ex-boyfriend who is still capable of manipulating you into fits of rage. Or it could even be a family member.

Of course, tolerance for toxicity is relative to each person; you have to decide when someone requires distance, and when they need to be cut out of your life. Those lines vary from person to person. For example, your sister will probably get more leeway than a co-worker, but everyone's sister and co-workers are different, and everyone has a different threshold.

What we're talking about here is true toxicity, the kind that infects, metastasizes, and takes over your life. Here are a few classic signs of toxic people.

Toxic people try to control you. Strange as it might sound, people who aren't in control of their own lives tend to want to control others. The toxic look for ways to control others, either through overt methods or subtle manipulation.

Toxic people disregard your boundaries. If you're always telling someone to stop behaving a certain way and they only continue, that person is probably toxic. Respecting the boundaries of others comes naturally to well-adjusted adults. The toxic person thrives on violating them.

Toxic people take without giving. Give and take is the lifeblood of true friendship. Sometimes you need a hand, and sometimes your friend does, but in the end, it more or less evens out. Not with the toxic person, they're often there to take what they can get from you, as long as you're willing to give it.

Toxic people are always "right", especially when they are not. They're going to find ways to be right even when they're not. They rarely (if ever) admit when they've messed up, miscalculated, or misspoken.

Toxic people aren't honest, and I'm not talking about natural exaggerations, face-saving or white lies here. I'm talking about blatant and repeated patterns of dishonesty.

Toxic people love to be victims. The toxic revel in being a victim of the world. They seek to find ways to feel oppressed, put down, and marginalized in ways they clearly are not. This might take the form of excuses, rationalizations, or out-and-out blaming.

Toxic people don't take responsibility. Part of the victim mentality comes from a desire to avoid responsibility. When the world is perpetually against them, their choices and actions can't possibly be responsible for the quality of their life; it's "just the way things are."

Do any of these sound familiar? They might help diagnose toxicity in the people around you, even if the toxic pattern isn't always or immediately obvious. In fact, toxicity can easily go unnoticed for years until you stop to consider your own experience of a difficult person. Though our thresholds for toxicity are relative, that's often because we fail to recognize the symptoms.

So how do you go about removing toxic people from your life?

Removing toxic people from your life is Important. It's rare for a toxic person to totally sabotage your self-improvement attempts, but it does happen. At the very least, they will certainly slow your progress. More to the point, would you want someone in your life who's actively opposed to making your life better?

The answer, of course, is no. And yet, that can be hard to accept until you begin to recognize the effects of toxicity within you.

Under the influence of a toxic person, you might second guess yourself on an important decision. You might feel sad, uncomfortable, and downright ashamed about your own progress and well-being. You might even take on some of the same toxic qualities you resent in others, something that happens to the best of us because toxic people have a peculiar way of making you toxic yourself.

And more often than not, the pattern happens without us even realizing. If you've ever had a toxic boss, then you know how this works: His behavior makes you irritable and bitter, so you lose your temper with the team working under you, which causes your employees to become increasingly difficult with one another, which causes them to bring that attitude home to their friends and family, and before you know it, the poison has unconsciously spread.

Don't feel like you owe them a huge explanation. Any explaining you do is more for you than for them. Again, tell them how you feel, which is a subject not open for debate. Or, if you prefer, keep it simple: Tell them calmly and kindly that you don't want them in your life anymore, and leave it at that. How much or how little you tell them is really up to you. Every relationship requires a different approach.

Talk to them in a public place. It's not unheard of for toxic people to get belligerent or even violent. Talking to them publicly can significantly diminish the chances of this happening. If you run into problems, you can just get up and leave.

Block them on social media. Technology makes distancing more difficult, so don't leave any window open for them to bully or cajole you. You've set boundaries. Stick to them. This includes preventing them from contacting you via social media, if appropriate. Shutting down email and other lines of communication with a toxic person might also be in order.

Don't argue. It's tempting to fall into the dynamic of toxicity by arguing or fighting, that is precisely what toxic people do. In the event they do return, make a promise with yourself to avoid an argument. Firmly restate your boundaries, then end communication. You're not trying to "debate" the person into leaving you alone. This isn't a negotiation. You can, however, make it less and less attractive for them to keep bothering you. "Do not feed the trolls!"

Consider writing a letter. Writing yourself a letter is a sort of dress rehearsal for an in-person conversation. You're clarifying your thoughts and articulating your feelings. You can also refer back to the letter later if you need to remember why you made the decision to cut someone out. Because toxic people often do everything they can to stay in your life, you'll need all the help you can get.

Consider creating distance instead of separation. Remember the person we talked about above, the one who's not toxic, but just a drag? You don't have to cut these people out of your life completely. You just need to create distance by occupying your time with other friends and activities and agreeing not to feed into their dynamic.

And in many cases, you might not have to "do" anything at all.

For many toxic relationships, especially with friends and colleagues, you'll only need to make an internal decision to create some space, without having a bigger conversation with the toxic person again. Remember: You don't owe anyone an explanation. You can just slowly ghost out of their life to the degree necessary until you're no longer affected by the toxicity That might seem obvious, but it can be tempting to think that you have to make your distancing obvious and vocal, when in fact most of the work is on your side of the equation. Like a fire, you can simply stop feeding the flames.

Still, there's one specific scenario in which you might have to handle things a little differently: when toxic people are your blood relatives.

WHAT IF THAT TOXIC PERSON IS A FAMILY MEMBER?

A toxic relative is a sticky situation. There are no easy answers and no standard answers that are right for everyone. Still, getting rid of toxic family members might be the most important cut you'll ever make. Family has a unique way of getting under your skin and directly influencing your thoughts, behaviors, and choices. Relatives don't own you simply by virtue of being blood. Being family doesn't confer any special exceptions to toxicity. Relatives don't have a magical license to screw up your life. Remember that.

This is why simply creating distance from toxic relatives is probably the best move, whether it's physical or emotional. But when it comes to family (as opposed to friends or colleagues), your distancing might require some special allowances. You might distance yourself emotionally, while still recognizing that you'll have to interact with this person on a practical level (by seeing them at holiday dinners, say, or taking care of a parent together). Indeed, your distancing with a family member might require you to disentangle your practical involvement from your emotional involvement. You'll still agree to engage with this person when necessary, but you'll refuse to let them drag you into the emotional pattern of toxicity.

119

The important thing with family is to tread lightly and make calm, rational decisions because how you deal with a toxic family member can color your entire family relationship. There are often larger ripple effects in a family than there are in a friendship or workplace.

Cutting people (especially family) out of your life can be one of the most challenging things you can do. But as we've said, it's also one of the most liberating and life-changing decisions you'll ever make.

Most importantly, cutting toxic people out sends a key message to yourself. You're saying: "I have value." You're prioritizing your happiness over someone else's dysfunction. Once you recognize how toxic people can erode this basic sense of self-worth, it becomes harder and harder to allow them in your life.

CAN YOU FIX A TOXIC PERSON?

We cannot fix a toxic person, although we hope to do so. It is impossible to control other people's behaviors. The best we can do is set an example through our actions. There is a possibility that if we set an example for people around us, people see our efforts and decide to become more like us, although there is no guarantee. Hence, our focus should be on ourselves and not necessarily on fixing the people around us.

WHAT IF A TOXIC PERSON WANTS TO COME BACK?

Letting a toxic person back into your life can be dangerous. When you let go of a toxic person, they might eventually see the value in your friendship and apologize for their behavior, promising that this will not happen again, and they want to be a part of your life. For the first time, give the other person a chance but set clear boundaries and be mindful when building back trust. If they exhibit any of the toxic behavior that they have in the past, they will lose you forever. Make sure to stand behind your words and show the other person that they cannot overstep your boundaries. While compassion is crucial, make sure you're putting yourself first and thinking about this person's effect on your life as well.

WHAT IF I'M A TOXIC PERSON AND I WANT TO CHANGE?

By recognizing your behavior, you've already completed the first step. If others gave you feedback about how you're hurting them, listen to the feedback that they are giving. Do not try to fight back with how they feel or what their claims are. Work on building self-compassion, as generally toxic people are toxic to people around them because they have a toxic relationship with themselves.

Try to see how you can work on your relationship with yourself, and that will carry over to other aspects of your life. Combine people's feedback with understanding who you are, and you will move away from being a toxic person and slowly cultivate high value.

MIND YOUR OWN BUSINESS

When someone around you has a toxic moment, in which they say something that is: Not nice, uncalled for, judgemental, unsolicited, "mood or vibe killing", remember not to entertain or engage with that behavior.

Remind yourself that if they are judging you about something is because they themselves are still working on their own flaws about that specific topic, they are judging you; therefore, they project it upon you because you have triggered them. You don't need to stay in that unhealthy environment, grab your things, and leave if you have to.

You don't need to feel the urge to educate them about that topic or find a need to validate yourself to them. You can literally ignore them, and with compassion, understand their own process, becoming unbothered as you continue to mind your own business.

At that moment that you want to say something back, maybe with anger, or maybe you feel you need to validate yourself to them remember:

- Reconnect with yourself again.
- Self-Validation is all you need.
- They are just projecting into you their own flaws.

- Whatever they think of you doesn't affect you.
- You are more than what anyone can perceive.
- You are loved and understood, and whoever doesn't get you or is aligned with your life doesn't deserve to experience you.
- You don't have to answer to anyone.

People see what they want to see. They don't know the season you are in, and you don't need to explain to them either. When you are unbothered, you don't feel the need to validate yourself to others.

ASK YOURSELF:

1. Who makes me feel unhappy or who never brings joy into my life?
2. Is someone I am helping bringing heavy weight into my life?
3. How do I feel when I am around them?
4. Who doesn't make me feel like that?
5. How will I know I no longer need that kind of person in my life?
6. How will I know I have let go of that toxic person out of my life?
7. Is the toxic person in my family? My parents?
8. What blowback will I get from other family members? What will the holidays be like? Can you realistically cut them out completely?
9. Have you ever had to cut a toxic person out of your life? How did you do it? What was the outcome?
10. How could it be better in the future?

PRINCIPLE 31

Let go of toxic people

PRINCIPLE 32

Mind your own business.

PRINCIPLE 33

Be Unbothered.

THE FEARS

> " *One of the greatest discoveries a man makes, one of his great surprises, is to find he can do what he was afraid he couldn't do.*"
>
> – Henry Ford

FEAR OF EXTINCTION

The fear of annihilation, of ceasing to exist. This is more than just a "fear of death" or how we might die - it strikes at the very heart of our fear that we would simply no longer be.

Dr. Albrecht calls it existential anxiety. It's the panicky feeling we get if we look over the edge of a tall building, or when we think too deeply about a deadly disease!

FEAR OF BEING INJURED OR MUTILATED

The fear of losing a part of our body, having our body's boundaries invaded, or of losing a natural function. This would be any fear where we feel physically unsafe or under attack.

FEAR OF LOSS OF AUTONOMY

The fear of being restricted, confined, trapped, suffocated. As Dr. Albrecht puts it, "the fear of being immobilized, paralyzed, restricted, enveloped, overwhelmed, entrapped, imprisoned, smothered, or otherwise controlled by circumstances beyond our control." When it's a physical fear, it's called claustrophobia, but our fear of being smothered, restricted, unable to take care of ourselves, or dependent on others can also apply to situations in our lives - or our relationships.

FEAR OF REJECTION, SEPARATION OR ABANDONMENT

The fear of abandonment, rejection - we humans have a strong need to belong. This is my biggest fear. From an evolutionary perspective, when an early human was kicked out of the tribe, they likely would have died. Dr. Albrecht refers to a "loss of connectedness; of becoming a non-person, not wanted, respected, or valued by anyone else," which literally threatens our wellbeing and survival.

FEAR OF EGO-DEATH

Humiliation, Shame, or Worthlessness. Dr. Albrecht called this type of fear, "Ego-death". We all need to feel lovable, worthy of love, and of value in the world order to have healthy relationships with others - and with ourselves. Shame can be an excruciating feeling - something many of us will go great lengths to avoid. Not only can it leave us feeling physically sick, make our skin crawl or flush, or in extremes give us stabbing pains, we want to crawl into a hole and disappear. When we are shamed and humiliated, it can threaten or destroy our belief in our worth, our lovability, and our value in the world. Without that, we are nobody. Literally. The supposed number 1 fear of public speaking would fall into this category!

FEAR OF SUCCESS

Fear of success also appears to be related to the level of control that the sufferer feels in his or her own life. Those who feel that external forces are in control tend to be at a higher risk for fear of success. It could be that they do not feel that their success has been earned, or it could be that they fear outside forces may take away their success.

Some people seem to fear both success and failure simultaneously. This can be a very difficult situation to be in, as every choice that the person makes must be weighed against these fears. It is entirely possible for someone in this situation to become paralyzed with indecision, unable to make any choices at all.

FEAR OF SELF-PROMOTION

The fear of self-promotion is often heavily interconnected with the fears of failure and success. Loosely defined as a type of social phobia, the fear of self-promotion can make it difficult or impossible to ask for a raise, seek a better job, or even land a first date. The fear of self-promotion is sometimes linked to imposter syndrome, a disorder hallmarked by feeling like a fraud, no matter how many accomplishments you make.

FEAR OF FAILURE

To find the causes of fear of failure, we first need to understand what "failure" actually means.

We all have different definitions of failure, simply because we all have different benchmarks, values, and belief systems. A failure to one person might simply be a great learning experience for someone else.

Many of us are afraid of failing, at least some of the time. But fear of failure is when we allow that fear to stop us from doing the things that can move us forward to achieve our goals.

Fear of failure can be linked to many causes. For instance, having critical or unsupportive parents is a cause for some people. Because they were routinely undermined or humiliated in childhood, they carry those negative feelings into adulthood.

Experiencing a traumatic event at some point in your life can also be a cause. For example, say that several years ago, you gave an important presentation in front of a large group, and you did very poorly. The experience might have been so terrible that you became afraid of failing in other things. And you carry that fear even now, years later.

STOP LIVING IN FEAR

If you are afraid of failure, you might be uncomfortable setting goals. But goals help us define where we want to go in life. Without goals, we have no sure destination. Many experts recommend visualization as a powerful tool for goal setting. Imagining how life will be after you've reached your goal is a great motivator to keep you moving forward.

However, visualization might produce the opposite results in people who have a fear of failure. Research shows that people who have a fear of failure were often left in a strong negative mood after being asked to visualize goals and goal attainment. So, what can you do instead? Start by setting a few small goals.

These should be goals that are slightly, but not overwhelmingly, challenging. Think of these goals as "early wins" that are designed to help boost your confidence. For example, if you've been too afraid to talk to the new department head (who has the power to give you the promotion you want), then make that your first goal. Plan to stop by her office during the next week to introduce yourself. Or, imagine that you've dreamed of returning to school to get your MBA, but you're convinced that you're not smart enough to be accepted into business school. Set a goal to talk with a school counselor or admissions officer to see what's required for admission.

Try to make your goals tiny steps on the route to much bigger goals. Don't focus on the end picture: getting the promotion or graduating with an MBA. Just focus on the next step: introducing yourself to the department head, and talking to an admissions officer. That's it.

Taking one small step at a time will help build your confidence, keep you moving forward, and prevent you from getting overwhelmed with visions of your final goal.

ASK YOURSELF:

1. Is there an experience that I am feeling and sensing in my memory that is associated with my fears?
2. Is fear stopping me from thriving in life?
3. When was the first time I was aware of that fear?
4. What is the best way I can work with my fears?
5. Are my fears bigger than me and I need professional help?
6. How will I know I have overcome my fears?

PRINCIPLE 34

Be fearless.

PART IV

ANCHOR YOUR JOY
FROM WITHIN

EMBRACE YOURSELF WITH LOVE

Respect yourself, love yourself, because there has never been a person like you and there never will be again."

– Osho

THE "DAVID" OF Michelangelo, the astonishing Renaissance sculpture, was created between 1501 and 1504. In 1501, Michelangelo was only 26 years old, and he was already the most famous and best-paid artist in his days. "David" was originally commissioned by the Opera del Duomo for the Cathedral of Florence. The project begun in 1464 by Agostino di Duccio and later carried on by Antonio Rossellino in 1475. Both sculptors had, in the end, rejected the enormous block of marble due to the presence of too many "taroli", or imperfections.

The single block of marble that was used to create "David" was neglected for 25 years until Michelangelo started working on it. He believed that the figure was already formed within the block of marble and that he only needed to take out what wasn't part of the figure of "David". Layer by layer, blower by blower, after four years of hard labor, he liberated "David" from his rocky prison.

The sculpture is already complete within the marble block, before I start my work. It is already there, I just chisel away the superfluous material." "Beauty is the purgation of superfluities".

– Michelangelo

Embracing who we are and loving ourselves is pretty much like that. It is not about accepting in our lives everything that society, what our family wants us to be, or the traumas that we inherited or learned. Embracing and loving ourselves is about knowing where we stand, who we are, and carving out of our lives what we are not.

131

Identifying and connecting with that metaphysical figure of you, your dreams, your goals, your beauty, your purpose, your thoughts, your spirit, and your body will help you identify what you are not. Respecting and honoring your body, loving your story, your journey, and every aspect of your life will bring nothing but joy to your life. It's like falling in love with yourself.

Turn off the TV and unplug from social media for 15 minutes to get centered, moisturize your skin with an intention, give your body some pleasure, some love. As you massage your feet, thank them for getting you to where you need to go. As you moisturize your hands, love them for all the quantum transactions, the way they are creative, introductions, and all they've done for you throughout your life. For a moment, stop taking your body for granted and immerse yourself in self-gratitude with your own body and your story.

Make lists about "What's Working for Me" and "What you love about yourself". Truly loving yourself comes from self-acceptance and self-validation. One helpful step toward getting to that point of self-acceptance is recognizing what you already have. Once you see it on paper, in your journal, and accept all of the positivity in your life, it will make it that much easier to love yourself.

Treating your body like a loving vessel will boost not only your self-love but also your energy. Be intentional about what you put into your body, not because you want to look good but because you want to feel good. Feeding your body nutrient-rich foods will have you oozing love out of every pore.

Tidying is more therapeutic than you might think, and getting rid of old things will make room for new ones to come into your life. Cleansing your mind can sometimes work in the form of letting go of clothes, shoes, jewelry, etc., that remind you of a certain time in your life that links to a low vibration. Don't chase what's already happened; love yourself enough to know the best is yet to come. Only when we love ourselves, we are committing to ourselves.

Do something you're good at is the ultimate self-esteem booster. Self-esteem and self-love often go hand in hand, and participating in a hobby, you're good at will not only boost your endorphins but will bring out the best version of you. If you love to cook, then cook! If you love to run, then grab those sneakers, head outside, and run. If you love to take a bath, gardening, painting, singing, dancing! Do whatever makes you happy!

FIND YOUR HAPPY PLACE

Think of a place that makes it simple to just be happy and allows you to joyfully enjoy life. Make a list in your journal about all these places that make you happy and visit them if you can. Make it unlimited!

ASK YOURSELF:

1. When was the first time that I felt self-love?
2. Has anyone in my life made me feel unloved?
3. How did I respond to those actions?
4. Did I love myself enough to not let that affect me back then?
5. What are five ways I can practice self-love in my everyday life?
6. In which places do I feel I am myself, and I am happy?
7. How often do I go to these places?
8. What's working for me in life?
9. When was the last time I "treated" myself?
10. What can I do today to love myself?

PRINCIPLE 35

Embrace yourself with Self-love.

PRINCIPLE 36

Seek your happy places.

PRINCIPLE 37

Commit to yourself.

THE INTENTION, THE PURPOSE, AND SELF-VALIDATION

> *When I was 5 years old, my mother always told me that happiness was the key to life. When I went to school, they asked me what I wanted to be when I grew up. I wrote down 'happy'. They told me I didn't understand the assignment, and I told them they didn't understand life."*
>
> – John Lennon

CONTINUING THE METAPHOR that joy and happiness is a beautiful flower that we all want to possess, lets recap:

First, we made sure our soil was fertile and learned about the process. Then we removed what didn't serve the quality of the soil anymore. Now the soil is ready for the seed, and that is the anchoring of your joy. It is important that your happiness is anchored to a substantial, real, genuine, and truthful aspect of your present that you can identify.

The strongest anchor point in someone's life is their purpose. There are millions of people living life without a sense of purpose. They live all their life fulfilling survival needs and reacting according to their presents needs without the awareness of a sense of inner guidance or direction in life. That doesn't mean their lives are purposeless; life will always give you a purpose, whether you are aware or not. It only means that their purpose in life was shaped by their family, society, or other external forces and not themselves.

When you are aware of your purpose in life, you will start seeing it every day everywhere you go.

HAVE A PURPOSE IN YOUR LIFE

Many people create a beautiful life for themselves because they curate their purpose in such an artistic and poetic way that is reflected in the life they live. A purpose cannot be about material things or external things out of your control.

Your purpose has nothing to do with what you should do (or not). It is not about being right or wrong. It has nothing to do with what your parents think. It has nothing to do with being rich, respected, or famous. It's not even about what you want or desire. Instead, your life purpose emanates clearly from your body-mind-spirit once it is free from behavioral patterns and the ego.

It becomes clear and your truth once you have reached peace within. Heal the pain, and you are free to co-create a new story in harmony with the oneness of life, which can guide you to thrive for the rest of your days.

Purpose is not a big, hairy, or audacious goal. Instead, it is the way you can be each and every moment of each and every day that brings the most of your potential into the world. It is the glue that connects your brilliance with what your community needs most. Something you love to do, and that makes you happy and joyful. Purpose is a conversation between your heart and the heartaches of the world. It is a bridge between your unique gifts and what the world wants most from you. You can't second guess it with your head, ego, or force it to be something it isn't with your hands. It may not be convenient, moneymaking, or safe. Many of your loved ones may not understand it. Some may resist it. Yet, it does not matter who thinks what about it. It is your truth and your very unique journey.

Having a purpose in life is everything. Since I was young, I was well aware of my dreams and my purpose.

Purpose is to the mind what the heart is to the body—a central point of ever-fluctuating energy which, without its constant beat, will leave you dead.

SELF-VALIDATION

Purpose is also understanding the value of yourself, to yourself. What makes you feel good is not a purpose. Purpose is the aspects of the mind that operate independently of any event or person that you encounter. Purpose is true ownership. We do not own material wealth, nor do we own people. We own our bodies; we own our minds. I am not sure we own our energy-consciousness. But we own our actions, ideas, and thoughts. They are actually the only thing that belongs to us. If you own your own mind, this is not about control of the mind; it's about understanding what that brilliant mind of yours needs, outside of external validation.

Most people struggle to validate their own minds, without the use of external sources of pleasure, or using conditional happiness. It's easy to forget that purpose exists because we all derive so much pleasure from the external world we live in. I would never ever say that one should forego external validation for internal validation. Both go hand in hand. But both must be in balance, or in check, for true happiness and joy we seek.

If you do not have a balance of self-validation and external validation, when bad things happen, or you feel sad or lonely or angry or depressed, you sink way below the watermark because you have no boat to float upon. It happens to almost all of us unless you come from a home where internal validation was strong. Most of us do not come from this.

Your purpose has to be a vehicle of self-validation and not external validation. How to activate self-validation?

Self-validation includes:

- Encouraging yourself.
- Acknowledging your strengths, successes, progress, and effort.
- Noticing and accepting your feelings.
- Prioritizing your needs.
- Treating yourself with kindness.
- Saying nice things to yourself.
- Accepting your limitations, flaws, and mistakes.

Things you can say to yourself:

- It's normal to feel this way.
- My feelings are valid.
- I'm proud of myself.
- This is hard. What do I need to do to cope or feel better?
- It's okay to cry.
- I'm making progress.
- I gave it my best effort.
- I am worthy.
- Good job! I'm more than my accomplishments or failures.
- My self-worth isn't based on other people's opinions.
- Everyone makes mistakes; that is how we learn to do things that are good.
- My feelings matter, and I will listen to what they're telling me.
- I trust my instincts and what my heart tells me.
- Not everyone likes me, and that's okay. I like myself.
- I like _____ about myself.

*Write in your journal things you like about yourself.

THE INTENTION

Once you have a sense of self-validation, from that space it is important to move with intention. That every action of yours, that you filter through the "Six elements of Behavior" has an intention. Having a purpose is literally giving an intention to your life as a whole. You can live your life filled with intentions in every action you take, everything you say, even when you drink water, and you will have a stronger impact with your actions. Have an intention with everything you do, an intention that is aligned with your purpose.

HOW DO I SET AN INTENTION?

Your intention should be closely tied to your personal thoughts, values, and perspective on life. Intentions can be a clear and specific wish, or as simple as a word or phrase you'd like to align yourself with, like "open your mind and heart," "love," "softness," "strength," "compassion for myself and others," "peace," or "freedom." Try to keep the intention positive, so instead of saying "stop being a coward," or "spend less time alone," choose the intentions, "be courageous" or simply, "community". Let your intention take action for your values.

CREATE YOUR PURPOSE

If your purpose is synthesized to a one-line statement is easier for you to remember it at all times, even though you can write a manifesto of your purpose as well. Your purpose can be vast, but if you keep it down to one sentence, you can make it part of your daily thoughts and have it available and easy to access in your thoughts.

Also, if we are making the "joyful leap", we need to state our purpose in the present tense, as if it is already here.

Here a few examples of how you can write the statement of your purpose. Your purpose can be synthesized within one sentence using, self-validation qualities, intentions, positive emotions, values, and addressing it for your ultimate wellbeing or for the planet. For example:

1. "My purpose is to create and validate myself with the joy the world has to offer."
2. "My purpose is to share my happiness with others."
3. "My purpose is to use my strengths and talents to spread joy on the planet."
4. "My purpose is to be happy."
5. "My purpose is to live joyfully, peacefully, and enlightened while using my talents and voice to inspire for a better world. "
6. "My purpose is to joyfully fulfill all my needs and the needs of my family."
7. "My purpose is to fulfill my joy by saving endangered species."
8. "My purpose is to joyfully explore all happiness the world has to offer."
9. "My purpose is to expand our idea of life on earth."
10. "My purpose is to be in peace, free, and to listen to my heart."

11. "My purpose is to be in love and share that love with every person I meet."
12. "My purpose is to highlight from my heart the beauty of the world."
13. "My purpose is to joyfully become a bridge between the earth and other planets."
14. "My purpose is to inspire for a peaceful and harmonious planet."
15. "My purpose is to strengthen my purpose every day with new reasons to be happy."

Everyone needs a purpose, but a purpose must come from internal validation and not external. To find a purpose is a lifelong endeavor, and your purpose might change through time and life experiences, but a purpose is important because it gives you guidance and a sense of direction towards a meaningful life.

Your purpose in life is to find purpose. That's what this life is really about. A sense of belonging brings meaning to once life. When we are understood, recognized, and affirmed by friends, family members, partners, colleagues, and even strangers, we feel we belong to a community. Many people count their relationships as the most meaningful part of their lives, even when those relationships are difficult or strained.

When we have long-term goals in life that reflect our values and serve the greater good, we tend to infuse our activities with more meaning. Researcher Adam Grant has found that professions focused on helping others like teachers, surgeons, clergy, and therapists, all tend to rate their jobs as more meaningful, and that people with purpose are more dedicated to their jobs. Choose a career that is aligned with your purpose, or that also serves your purpose. Remember to align your purpose with your career. It wouldn't make sense if your purpose involves transforming farm agriculture, but you work as an accountant for a corporate job. You will probably be unhappy. Take the risks you need to take and go after that job that is truly aligned with your purpose.

Having purpose has also been tied to many positive outcomes, including increased learning for students in school and better health. When it comes to finding meaning, our life story is meant to be told in a coherent narrative that defines our identity and purpose. People who describe their lives as meaningful tend to have redemptive stories where they overcame something negative or low, and to emphasize growth, communion with others, and personal agency.

Experiences that fill us with awe or wonder, the ones that expand our enlightenment, the ones in which we feel we have risen above the everyday world to experience a higher reality, can decrease our self-focus and lead us to engage in more generous, helpful and purposeful behavior with our communities.

THE "I AM" EXERCISE

Write a list of all the things that you are, starting with "I am". Example, I am joyful, I am positive, etc.

ASK YOURSELF:

1. Who am I?
2. What is the purpose of my life? What makes my life meaningful?
3. Over the last seven days, what moments have given you feelings of great love, deep satisfaction, or purpose?
4. Over the last month, when have I felt most switched on? What was I doing? Who was I back then?
5. Over the last six months, when did I feel most alive and electrified? What was I doing? Who was I back then?
6. What are the greatest challenges I have encountered in my life? In overcoming them, what talents, gifts, and ideas did I develop?
7. What do I want my grandkids to say about me?
8. Letting go of any should or musts, thinking across an average day, what activities most inspire me?
9. What about when I was a kid before any seriousness or ambition snuck in? Which memories most electrify my body and mind when I think of them?
10. If I have been put on this planet by aliens to use all my insights, experiences, and gifts to bring more love to the world, what would I do each day?

11. If I never had to work again and everybody adored me as I am, what would I spend my days doing to feel most fulfilled and most alive?
12. What matters most to me?
13. What would I like to build, create, or nurture in my life?
14. How do I feel when I am my happiest self?
15. What makes me proud?
16. What word(s) would I like to align myself with?
17. What fears would I like to release?
18. What am I grateful for today?
19. How can I self-validate my life every day?
20. Which activities can I do to self-validate my life?
21. What are my goals in life?
22. Which new goals can I set in my life that are aligned with my purpose?
23. Does my mind require space, free thought, relaxation?
24. How does my mind create this, or how do my actions allow for this?
25. Do I ever take the time to think about what is important for me, outside of extrinsic needs?
26. How are my actions impacting the world?

PRINCIPLE 38

Self-validation over outside validation.

PRINCIPLE 39

Live a meaningful and purposeful life.

PRINCIPLE 40

Have an intention for all of your actions.

PRINCIPLE 41

Be at the service of the wellbeing of the planet.

PRINCIPLE 42

Have goals in life.

PRINCIPLE 43

Align your purpose with your career.

BELIEVE IN YOURSELF

As soon as you trust yourself, you will know how to live."
-Johann Wolfgang von Goethe

WHAT DOES "BELIEVE in yourself" mean? Believing in yourself has two core components. The first is a solid belief in your inherent value as a human being; it's the deep-down understanding that you are someone with gifts to offer the world and who recognizes that you mattered important the moment you were born. This is self-worth, and also self-validation.

The second is confidence. Merriam-Webster defines confidence as,

A feeling or consciousness of one's power or reliance on one's circumstances, and also as the quality or state of being certain."

I look at confidence as the willingness to step up and be seen and heard, even in the face of uncertainty, even when you're frightened to do so or without money or expensive outfits.

Self-approval and self-acceptance in the now are the main keys to positive changes in every area of our lives."
– Louise L. Hay

You are Important, and you matter. You Can't Change That. Loving, validating, and approving yourself has nothing to do with the ego. It has to do with you acknowledging your ideas, gifts, life, and the universe's power within you: a beautiful and unique expression of life. When you think of important people in your life, do you count yourself among them?

When you don't believe in yourself, you often end up trapped in harsh self-judgment instead of embracing gentle self-acceptance. You become either unwilling or unable to express your vulnerability. It is our vulnerability that makes us better able to connect more authentically and more lovingly with others.

Ultimately, learning to believe in yourself requires you to start looking at yourself through the lens of unconditional self-acceptance and embracing every aspect of you.

*Get more mirrors in your home so you can be reminded more often of how beautiful you are.

ASK YOURSELF:

1. What have I accomplished in your life so far?
2. What have I learned from those moments?
3. Did I believe in myself in those moments?
4. In which ways am I not believing in myself right now?
5. Do I think my ideas are crazy or unevaluable?
6. Did somebody make me feel that way?
7. Who makes me doubt myself?
8. Why is that? Are they projecting something on me, or is it me projecting something on them?
9. How will I know I believe in myself?

PRINCIPLE 44

Believe in Yourself, in your dreams, in your purpose.

PRINCIPLE 45

Be confident, no matter what.

HONESTY IS THE BEST POLICY

W HAT IS TRUE for you always exists at the core of you. While everything else around you may change on a dime, what is authentic and true is immutable. If you're going to rely on anything to get you through life, shouldn't it be that constant?

When you are connected to your core truth, your purpose, and values, you aren't affected by others' negative opinions of you. You know who you are, and don't believe you need to change that. You also don't feel the need to judge others or gossip about them, as your security makes you accepting of yourself and others.

If you build your identity on the fluctuating foundation of public opinion and "fashion du jour," nothing will be constant. And if nothing is constant, nothing will be reliable. In order to pursue what you want, you have to be able to rely on yourself. Not millions of people you don't know. Yourself.

Again, this is about planting your truth at the core of your being and growing your passions from there. When you have something meaningful, that is "always there for you," you become empowered. Let that meaningful and constant thing be you.

Being honest with yourself is as essential to being honest with others. No relationship can survive, let alone thrive, without honesty. And if you are hiding your truth from yourself, how will you ever find it to share it with someone else? Relationships that are healthy, happy, and balanced are comprised of people who are in touch with their authentic selves, and this authentic self-connection is reflected in effective and honest communication.

Being honest with yourself leads to feelings of openness, expansion, inner joy, and freedom. When your physical core is strong and stable, your entire body is stronger and more fluid. The same is true for your spiritual and emotional core. When that is stable, the rest of your life is free to be expansive.

Honesty provides clarity. Lies will always keep you stuck and only hurt the person holding them. When you are honest with yourself, you will always know what you need to do, even if that is difficult. You will make wiser decisions about relationships and jobs and will more immediately avoid those situations that don't serve you.

Being honest with yourself increases personal responsibility for both your choices and their consequences. Acceptance of responsibility is foundational to changing your life in a positive way. Changing is then not simply "changing," it is evolving, expanding, and making a quantum leap. As you evolve, the world responds by offering you new opportunities to understand yourself.

As you stand firmly in your own truth, the life that once had you hiding behind public opinion becomes beautiful, and you realize that you are a work of art, unique with values, passion, and purpose and that my friend is integrity. You are integrated within your truth with love.

ASK YOURSELF:

1. Do I lie to myself or others?
2. If so, when was the first time I did so?
3. Am I living a life based on pretending to be something I am not?
4. Am I really being honest with every action of my life?
5. Why do I feel I need to believe I am something else from who I am when I am beautiful?
6. How will I know I am being honest with myself?
7. What would need to happen for me to know?

PRINCIPLE 46

Be honest with yourself and others.

KNOW YOUR VALUES

VALUES ARE A broad concept that guides decisions in life. They determine what is important for each person, as they are the foundation of someone's character. Values are a set of internal filters that determines an individual model of the world. You can learn to recognize your values, align, and change values for self, others, groups, or organizations.

WHAT IS A VALUE SYSTEM?

Values or principles are your personal positions, something that you value highly and will not give up on. Once your value system becomes known, you set a certain consistency of behavior. Introducing consistency in expectation and behavior. People will get to know you and your boundaries and would know ahead of time certain decisions based on your value system. They would avoid bringing anything to you for a decision, which they know you will not approve of. You won't even have to fight such cases, and you will be protecting your happiness without even trying.

More importantly, it builds character and your "brand". For example, if you have established a good track record in working effectively with cross-cultural teams, and build certain principles around that, the next time such an initiative comes about, you will be a front-runner for leading those types of initiatives. A solid value system helps build trust around you. People around you know that you will stand for something based on your values and admire you for that.

Individuals with strong value systems are seen as an inspiring source of strength and naturally attract followers. Transitioning to leadership becomes a logical, consequential, and natural next step.

Some examples of values are:

- Family
- Friends
- Health
- Spirituality
- Mindfulness
- Learning
- Traveling
- Exploring
- Healthy Eating
- Wisdom
- Geography
- Economics
- Happiness
- Courage
- Joyful Leaps
- Temperance
- Sustainability
- Community

Examples of values according to Chris Howard studies:

Adventure, Authority, Authenticity, Being Active, Being in the moment, Being the best, Candor, Charisma, Cleanliness, Communication, Country, Creativity, Devotion, Duty, Efficiency, Excellence, Faith, Fame, Family, Fortune, Forward Thinking, Freedom, Friendship, Fulfilment, Fun, Godliness, Harmony, Health, Helping people, Helping the Environment, Homelife, Honesty, Humor, Integrity, Intelligence, Intimacy, Knowledge, Leadership, Leisure, Living Life to the fullest, Love, Loyalty, Making people laugh, Making people think, Order, Partnership, Passion, Peace, Perfection, Perseverance, Power, Precision, Punctuality, Purpose, Quality, Recognition, Self-awareness, Self-expression, Service, Sexuality,

Spirituality, Stability, Strength, Systems, Team playing, Transformation, Travel, Truth, Walking the talk, Wealth, Winning.

> *I further affirm that he who desires to be happy must pursue and 'practice temperance and run away from intemperance as fast as his legs will carry him."*
>
> – Socrates

HOW TO BUILD YOUR OWN VALUE SYSTEM?

It all begins with selecting one or a few values that you want to practice, perfect and, above all, proclaim to have. You can cheat and pick something that you either have or one that will come easy to you. I'd advise that you pick something that takes you out of your safe zone as well.

List them all in your journal. The next step is to put some measurements around it since you can only improve what you can measure. Look for every opportunity to practice it and then evaluate yourself against your target.

The key is to monitor, measure, and keep improving. Compare all your actions and make sure they are aligned with your values. Before you know it, the few values that you have practiced will speak on its own about your character and integrity.

ASK YOURSELF:

1. What are the top twenty-things that I value in life?
2. In order from the most important to the least important, how would that go?
3. Are my actions aligned with my value system?
4. Is my value system serving my purpose, goals, and dreams?
5. Am I willing to scarify my values to try to "fit in"?

6. If yes, why would I scarify my values, what I believe, and who I am just to "fit in"?
7. How will I know I am grounded in my values?

PRINCIPLE 47

Know your values.

BELIEFS SYSTEMS

There is no alternative to action, and that requires faith. The issue is how we are to mold for ourselves a belief system that is worthy of life."

– Naguib Mahfouz

I F A VALUE is what is important to us, a belief is what we trust to be true in the perception of our experience on earth. Your belief system is the invisible force behind your behavior. Together with other factors such as your personality and values, your cultural background and upbringings, your genetic setup, and your habits, your belief system is one of the strongest forces that affect any decision that you are making, even being happy. The communication styles you are using. The ways in which you react to any things that happen in your life. Any aspect of your behavior, really.

We gain them through things that other people say to us, things we hear on the news, things we read, or any other external influences that we are exposed to. These beliefs are interacting with one another, affecting one another, and forming a system.

These beliefs are interconnected with one another. A change in one belief will affect the system as a whole. If it is a core belief, a change can potentially lead to the disruption of the system as a whole. If a set of beliefs changes, other parts of the system will have to rearrange in order to rebuild the coherence of the system.

The ultimate goal of any belief system is to ensure human survival and to hold the individual spiritually and philosophically, the truth that will serve to understand the experience on the planet.

Intelligence and culture have developed as a way for humans to evolve faster, not on a physical level, but on a mental level. Cultural evolution happens much quicker than biological evolution. Belief systems have evolved as part of this development in order to ensure the survival of human beings.

For example, beliefs around sexuality and dating behavior are meant to ensure the passing of an individual's genes onto the next generation.

Beliefs around effective decision-making, negotiation, and business exist in order to help you achieve a certain financial status or in the social hierarchy.

Beliefs around dealing with things like uncertainty and anxiety exist in order to help you maintain mental health and so on and so forth.

In very drastic circumstances, your core beliefs get affected. Core beliefs are those which are at the very center of your own sense of self. Those beliefs that are so central to who you are, that putting them into question would mean that you even start to question who you are at the core of your being.

Culture shock, for example, is the condition that describes such a situation upon entering a different cultural environment. It describes a situation where we are exposed to such a drastically different worldview so suddenly and on such a large scale that we are forced to start questioning some of the most central assumptions which we had made about life so far.

A disruption of your belief system is a chance for growth. When we are facing a situation where our belief system gets disrupted so strongly that we are facing very negative emotions for a long time, we tend to think that there is something wrong with us.

Facing a long period of low emotions doesn't necessarily have to be a sign that you are a negative person. It can simply be a result of external influences that have caused you to question some of your core beliefs, which has subsequently caused a disruption of your belief system, and you haven't found the answers yet. It is important you answer the questions that are orbiting your thoughts and write them down in your journal with the intension of finding an answer to it.

Once you do that, it will take time for you to process this new information to the point where it becomes integrated into your belief system. Eventually, your existing beliefs will rearrange themselves in a way that the system reaches congruence once again, and you will have positive emotions again.

People who think that something is wrong with them start trying to 'get rid' of these negative feelings. They don't give themselves the space to process the new information and integrate it into their existing belief system. As a result, they develop a long-term identity crisis.

People who see the new information and new beliefs as a threat will often continue to reject it altogether. In doing so, they do not open up the space for themselves to absorb this new information and therefore continue to have strong, negative feelings for a long period of time. So, chill out and project your happiness by also not being so rigid with your beliefs when communicating with others.

When we embrace the pain of the process and simply let it be, we give our brain space to unconsciously work on the integration of the new beliefs into our belief system, and the rearrangement of existing beliefs in ways that make a synthesis between two different viewpoints possible. Even if these different viewpoints are so contradictory that it seems impossible on the first view. Writing in your journal is the number one thing I recommend to help process new information. Write it down, ask new questions, find new answers.

That is when real personal growth happens. When we start becoming a significantly different person than who we used to be. When our beliefs change so drastically that people around us start to wonder why we have changed so much in such a short period of time. Maybe within even 22 days. Be mindful of which beliefs are yours and which are not, or part of the collective unconscious beliefs.

THREE KEY ELEMENTS OF A BELIEF SYSTEM:

HOMEOSTASIS:

Belief systems are constantly striving towards reaching a state of equilibrium. This is a state in which the elements of the system only have contradictions that do not affect the stability of the system as a whole—a state of relative congruence.

SELF-REGULATION:

Belief systems have the capability to adapt themselves to the external conditions in which they are placed. In that sense, the system is capable of reaching a state of congruence regardless of the circumstances through a constant feedback mechanism between internal beliefs and external factors.

AUTOPOIESIS:

Belief systems are capable of reproducing and maintaining themselves. This goes beyond the capability of mere self-regulation in the sense that it has the ability to change quite significantly and become significantly more complex as part of this process.

Expose yourself to a completely different kind of environment. Join a community that is very different from what you are used to. Move to another country or state. Take on a job in a completely different field than you were trained in. Read books about a topic that you normally would've never touched.

For most people, their belief system is this invisible force that is influencing their behavior without them noticing. Become aware of how your beliefs affect your behavior and consciously shape how your belief system develops. Your behavior and your habits will follow.

WHEN DISAGREEING WITH SOMEONE WITH A DIFFERENT BELIEF SYSTEM

Remember that there is duality in the universe, and sometimes we experience it even in conversations we engage in. Always show respect for the other person's opinions, think of it as valid as yours. Never say, "you are wrong". The best way of winning an argument is by avoiding it and therefore protecting your joy. Practice being unbothered. You cannot pretend to go around in life telling people what they should believe in, that is everyone's right to freely decide. You can have a conversation and express your beliefs with facts, but always have a focus on finding the common ground and appreciate the duality. Show real appreciation about their beliefs.

Instead, say,

> *I respect your opinion about this topic, and I can understand you feel like that about it..."*

Then find a belief system that you both agree and link it to your perspective on the topic. For example,

> *We both agree that disagreeing enforces our freedom, and that is precisely why I think that our common ground is that we both want this... (insert another common belief)..."*

ASK YOURSELF:

1. What are the top 10 truths that are part of what I consider my core belief system?
2. Which one is the most important?
3. How did I become aware of that belief for the first time?
4. How did I learn that to be the truth? From my family member, a friend, a social behavior?
5. Have I questioned that belief to be true, or have I assumed is the truth?
6. Are my beliefs aligned and in harmony with my purpose?
7. Are my beliefs in synchronicity with my values?

8. How do my beliefs make me feel?
9. Do I constantly have a friction of beliefs with anyone in my life? Why?
10. How do I engage in a dispute with that person?
11. Do I make them feel their opinion matters and is appreciated?
12. How will I know I am in peace with my beliefs?
13. Have I ever had conversations with loved ones, friends aligning values, and beliefs?

PRINCIPLE 48

Know your beliefs.

PRINCIPLE 49

Avoid arguments and telling people what to believe in.

IDENTIFY YOUR STRENGTH, OPPORTUNITY, AND ROOM TO GROW

SWOT

NOW THAT YOU'VE defined your purpose and self-love, career aspirations and goals, reevaluated your values and beliefs, the next step is to understand more about yourself and your external environment and professional life. This is where the SWOT analysis is helpful. It stands for:

S = Strengths (internal)

W = Weaknesses (internal)

O = Opportunities (external)

T = Threats (external)

This process captures information about your internal strengths and weaknesses as well as external opportunities and threats. The key to completing your SWOT analysis is to treat your career as a business and yourself as a competitive product.

STRENGTH

To help you understand your strengths, picture yourself as a competitive product in the marketplace. A personal strength is an asset to your gifts as a product and can be used as a way to differentiate yourself from others when interviewing, when in a meeting, or trying to obtain your next promotion. Examples of strengths: Strong project management skills, ability to improve or reengineer processes, experience, and training in presenting to large audiences, proven successful sales abilities.

WEAKNESS

A personal weakness is a liability or an area of opportunity for growth. These are characteristics you could improve upon to increase future job opportunities. Examples: Disorganized, uncomfortable speaking in front of groups, tendency to procrastinate, a poor listener.

OPPORTUNITIES AND THREATS

When thinking about your opportunities and threats, I always find it easier to begin with the "threats." Try comparing yourself to people you'll likely compete against for that next job or promotion. Then, as objectively as possible, judge your threats and determine possible ways to overcome them.

Here are some examples:

Threat: Other candidates have master's degrees.

Opportunity: Gain skills that match theirs (certified) or go and get a master's degree.

Threat: Colleague X is much better at presenting in front of groups.

Opportunity: Take a speech class or communication class (such as NLP).

You might find useful opportunities in the following: Networking events, educational classes, or conferences. There are opportunities that you will be even able to create for yourself, like starting your own company or creating a need that you can supply the demand for.

The purpose of the personal SWOT analysis is to identify actions you can take to best meet the requirements of the job or promotion you are seeking. Comparing your strengths and weaknesses to the job requirements will identify gaps and help you prepare to be the best candidate for the position or dream job to which you aspire.

You can use the SWOT analysis every time you're applying and interviewing for a new job, business meeting, and this tool is helpful in life as a whole! I have used the SWOT when having big investors meetings for my film or music projects, and with clients. Going through this exercise helps to anticipate areas that could be potential issues during the interview or meeting.

ASK YOURSELF:

Strength

1. What do you do well?
2. What do others see as my strength?
3. What unique resources can you draw on?
4. What advantages do you have that others don't have (for example, skills, certifications, education, or connections)?
5. What do you do better than anyone else?
6. Which of your achievements are you most proud of?
7. What values do you believe in that others fail to exhibit?
8. Are you part of a network that no one else is involved in? If so, what connections do you have with influential people?

Weakness

1. What could you improve?
2. Where do you have fewer resources than others?
3. What are others likely to see as my weakness?
4. What tasks do you usually avoid because you don't feel confident doing them?
5. Are you completely confident in your education and skills training? If not, where are you weakest?
6. What are your negative work habits (for example, are you often late, are you disorganized, do you have a short temper, or are you poor at handling stress)?

7. Do you have personality traits that hold you back in your field? For instance, if you have to conduct meetings on a regular basis, a fear of public speaking would be a major weakness.
8. Which weakness can become an opportunity?

Opportunities

9. What opportunities are open to you now? How can you turn your strength into opportunities?
10. What trends can you take advantage of?
11. What new technology can help you?
12. Or can you get help from others or from people via the internet?
13. Is your industry growing? If so, how can you take advantage of the current market?
14. Do you have a network of strategic contacts to help you, or offer good advice?
15. Is there a need in your company or industry that no one is filling?
16. Do your customers or vendors complain about something in your company? If so, could you create an opportunity by offering a solution?
17. Which opportunity can lead to strength?
18. A new role or project that forces you to learn new skills, like public speaking or international relations. A company expansion or acquisition. Do you have specific skills (like a second language) that could help with the process?

Threats

19. Do you feel you are your own obstacle? If so, explain why.
20. What obstacles do you currently face at work?
21. Which obstacles might others perceive I face?
22. Are any of your colleagues competing with you for projects or roles?
23. Is your job (or the demand for the things you do) changing?
24. Does changing technology threaten your position?
25. Could any of your weaknesses lead to threats?
26. Which threats can become an opportunity?

PRINCIPLE 50

Know your strength.

PRINCIPLE 51

Know your weakness.

PRINCIPLE 52

Know your opportunity.

PRINCIPLE 53

Know your flaws.

EXPRESS YOURSELF

> *If you bring forth what is within you, what you bring forth will save you. If you do not bring forth what is within you, what you do not bring forth will destroy you."*
>
> – Gospel of Thomas

EXPRESSING YOURSELF WILL make you so happy. Sometimes there is a big gap between who one is and what one does.

You could be a boss, an employee, a manager, a mother, a daughter, a celebrity, an influencer, and so on. Do these roles allow you to express who you truly are? Do your roles allow you to express your deeply held values? Are you expressing the full spectrum of life?

Imagine that life is a grand piano keyboard. Each note represents a different experience, a different possibility.

There are emotions like despair, anger, sadness, happiness, joy, bliss, and so on. There are states of clarity, wisdom, euphoria, inspiration. Of course, there are also negative states like depression and emptiness, and hopelessness. Then you also have values like love, courage, beauty, compassion, and discipline. But we do not express the fullness of life in our daily lives. While life offers us 88 notes, we are singing a 5-note song.

The truth is, we express only the parts of ourselves that get approval and recognition. When I was a child, I would usually get into trouble every time I would fully express myself to my parents. To make things worse, I had a very emotionally shy mother and very emotionally expressive father. I grew up in a very religious and conservative household; my parents' values and beliefs sometimes interfered with how I wanted to express myself as a child. I repressed that side of me unconsciously, but deep inside, I knew who I was from a very young age.

The part of me that was independent and had its own desires grew silent, but every now and then it would come out, I would fully express myself, and it would get me in trouble. It wasn't until I became an independent young man; I was able to fully express myself and explore my real voice.

Many people have silenced their voices forever because of their family or their environment, and then we wonder why we are unhappy and unfulfilled. You can't be silenced. If you do not act upon your dreams, what happens to your desires? If you do not say what you need to say, what happens to your words? If you do not cry when you need to, what happens to your tears?

The unexpressed parts of you do not simply disappear. They remain within you, and if you don't express them, they will explode one day in a very unexpected way (maybe even dangerous way).

BE YOU!

Allow yourself to express yourself, just as you are. It is time to bring forth all that is within you. You are perfect at this very moment. It is not about the perfection of your expression.

It is about having the courage to be who you are, and to know deep within your being that you are beautiful just are you are.

Discover and express yourself. You can work on your self-expression by expressing yourself creatively. These forms of expression require you to take a risk. There is no right or wrong, only what you express in the moment.

I love expressing myself with the songs I sing. I express myself through the images and videos I create, words I write, the information I process and share, and everything I utter out of my body from my heart.

Let your voice shine. Don't keep all your feelings bottled up. Don't keep all your words within. Your throat is a pressure valve for your body, where your inner truth takes form in the world through sound. The sound of your voice frees up your inhibitions so that your emotions can find expression in the world. With music, you are free from the conventions of everyday speech. You have a blank check to be yourself, truly. If you're interested in vocal coaching/singing lessons, find a tutor or learn it yourself.

Let your body speak and dance! You don't need to impress anyone, the only person you need to impress is yourself. Your body has a wisdom of its own, ancient wisdom. Your body stores your unexpressed emotions. Let it show you the way. Let yourself go, surrender to your instincts. Celebrate the primacy of dance and the immediacy of physical expression. Feel the energy shoot through your legs, your chest, your hands. Turn on the music and go! Find somewhere to dance freely. Learn about your natural rhythms and your feelings through your faithful body, your physical home.

You can also write! As you write, you discover all that is unsaid within you. You find thoughts you never knew you had. You find emotions you never knew you had. You gain access to your own depths. You gain access to your own wisdom. Let your words pour forth. Write and write and write, whatever comes to your mind. Keep writing and writing until you feel satisfied. Keep writing until your deepest desires make themselves known.

Meet yourself on paper between the letters. You can also try any other creative endeavor, like cooking, painting, talking out loud, gardening.

The more you express, the more you discover. The more you discover yourself, the more you express who you really are.

ASK YOURSELF:

1. Create my own expression. To truly express who I am in the world, without copying a pre-existing role. Who am I? What do I like? How do I like to feel?
2. What do I want to express? What brings me joy?
3. Is anyone in my life discouraging me from expressing myself? Or did anyone in my past?
4. How did I overcome that experience?
5. Am I currently expressing myself? Why?

6. How will I know I am expressing myself?
7. Why have I not fully expressed myself in the past? Why don't we express ourselves fully, in all our glory and fallibility? Why do we only show a part of ourselves?
8. How does the song of my heart sound?
9. Deep within my energy, there is a dance. How does it flow?
10. Deep within my soul, there is a rhythm. How does it beat?

PRINCIPLE 54

Be brave and express yourself.

HUMILITY FEEDS GRATITUDE

Gratitude is a quality similar to electricity: It must be produced and discharged and used up in order to exist at all."

– William Faulkner

GRATITUDE IS OFTEN spoken of as the starting point to creating a more successful life. In simple terms, when you first wake up in the morning, if you give thanks for the good things which are in your life, you will start the day off on a positive note, that will flow through the day. Make this routine a habit, and you will find this positive attitude becoming a part of who you are.

The ability to be truly grateful for the things in your life requires a core of humility. Humility seeds, feeds, and grows gratitude. Without a core of humility, I believe gratitude will always be superficial. Humility is really a powerful virtue and value, but unfortunately, it is not very popular today. With the 'me' culture that is so prevalent through social media and many of our societies and workplaces today, humility is seen as a weakness of surrendering and letting others get their way ahead of you.

A truly humble person can easily identify and accept that all the good things that are happening in their life are a 'blessing' for which they should be thankful. They don't have to prove to themselves or anyone else that it was their efforts that yielded the reward or outcome.

ASK YOURSELF:

1. Are you someone who wakes with an attitude of gratitude?
2. Could you start thinking about the good things that happen in your life each day?

3. What would you write on a list of 20 reasons you are grateful?
4. What would you write on a list of 20 reasons to be humble?
5. Are you able to open yourself to being humble?
6. How will you know you are humble?
7. Can you become a positive influence in your workplace/ community that encourages and supports others?
8. What are you grateful for today?

PRINCIPLE 55

Be humble.

PRINCIPLE 56

Be grateful.

PART V

THE OUTSIDE WORLD AND THE OTHERNESS

THE ENVIRONMENT

> *You are who you hang out with and are what you eat, you are where you go, you are the information you choose to absolve."*
>
> – Anonymous

B EHAVIOUR, CONDUCT, AND emotional patterns not only depend on epigenetic, but it also depends on the environment and energy field. Consider the impact of the parents and the family environment on personality. One might expect children who are raised by the same parents in the same way in the same home to turn out similar, but this fact isn't necessarily the case.

The environment is a crucial piece of the puzzle when you look at behavior because your brain and energy react profoundly to their surrounding environment. One of the main reasons you are not simply predestined for a particular behavior by your genes is that your environment can turn those genes on or off; when you learn how to optimize your environment, you learn how to make behavioral change easier and more successful.

In a way, we adapt to our environment and serve a purpose to it. If we are in a toxic environment, we will certainly play a role in that ecosystem. If you want to drastically change your life and make the quantum leap, to achieve quantum joyfulness, you must change your environment.

Your environment, which includes your family, friends, colleagues, location, habits, and lifestyle, impacts you far more, for better or for worse, than you realize. You can't make a significant, lasting change without altering some elements of your environment.

No place is inherently good or bad, but you should pay attention to how you feel while you're within those spots and note if that feeling changes when you leave them. Are you motivated or drained? If it's the latter, and you want to make drastic progress, it's time to make big changes.

ASK YOURSELF:

1. Who are the top 5 people of my life?
2. How do they make me feel?
3. Where do I hang out, and how do I feel while I am there?
4. Are my current environments aligned with my purpose, values, beliefs, and goals?
5. Which environments in my life are healthy for me?
6. Which environments in my life are not aligned with my joy?

PRINCIPLE 57

To make the joyful leap change your environment.

COMMUNICATION

Wise men speak because they have something to say; Fools because they have to say something."

– Plato

E FFECTIVE COMMUNICATION IS about more than just exchanging information. It's about understanding the emotion and intentions behind the information while also activating the emotional radar. As well as being able to clearly convey a message, you need to also listen in a way that gains the full meaning of what's being said and makes the other person feel heard and understood.

Effective communication sounds like it should be instinctive. But all too often, when we try to communicate with others, something goes astray. We say one thing, the other person hears something else, and misunderstandings, frustration, and conflicts arise. This can cause problems, frustrations, and sadness with your family & friends, school, social groups, and work relationships. Communicating effectively can lead to strong bonding and understandings that can bring joy and happiness to your life.

For many of us, communicating more clearly and effectively requires learning some important skills. Whether you're trying to improve communication with your spouse, kids, boss, or co-workers, learning these skills can deepen your connections to others, build greater trust and respect, and improve teamwork, problem-solving, and your overall social and emotional health. Consider someone else's perspective to build your thoughts from that space. Also:

CALM DOWN & BREATHE

When you're stressed or emotionally overwhelmed, you're more likely to misread other people, send confusing or off-putting nonverbal signals, and lapse into unhealthy knee-jerk patterns of behavior. To avoid conflict and misunderstandings, you can learn how to quickly calm down before continuing a conversation. You can remain silent until you have something wise to say from that space of calmness.

FOCUS

Lack of focus can also lead to unhealthy communication patterns. You can't communicate effectively when you're multitasking. If you're checking your phone, planning what you're going to say next, or daydreaming, you're almost certain to miss nonverbal cues in the conversation. To communicate effectively, you need to avoid distractions and stay focused.

BECOME AN ENGAGED LISTENER

When communicating with others, we often focus on what we should say. However, effective communication is less about talking and more about listening. Listening well means not just understanding the words or the information being communicated, but also understanding the emotions the speaker is trying to convey.

There's a big difference between engaged listening and simply hearing. When you really listen, when you're engaged with what's being said, you'll hear the subtle intonations in someone's voice that tell you how that person is feeling and the emotions they're trying to communicate. When you're an engaged listener, not only will you better understand the other person, you'll also make that person feel heard and understood, which can help build a stronger, deeper connection between you.

As strange as it sounds, the left side of the brain contains the primary processing centers for both speech comprehension and emotions. Since the left side of the brain is connected to the right side of the body, favoring your right ear can help you better detect the emotional nuances of what someone is saying.

Avoid interrupting or trying to redirect the conversation to your concerns, making their story about yours. We all know this kind of person; they make every conversation about themselves, even if you haven't even expressed your emotions. They also love saying something like, "If you think that's bad, let me tell you what happened to me." Listening is not the same as waiting for your turn to talk. You can't concentrate on what someone's saying if you're forming what you're going to say next. Often, the speaker can read your facial expressions and know that your mind's elsewhere.

Show your interest in what's being said. Nod occasionally, smile at the person and make sure your posture is open and inviting. Encourage the speaker to continue with small verbal comments like "yes" or "uh-huh."

Try to set aside all judgment, regardless of what they are saying is different from your values and beliefs, listen politely, and without judgment, because that is not your experience. In order to communicate effectively with someone, you don't have to like them or agree with their ideas, character, or opinions. However, you do need to set aside your judgment and withhold blame and criticism in order to fully understand them. The most difficult communication, when successfully executed, can often lead to an unlikely connection with someone. When you are talking with someone you disagree, the most you can do is inspire them with a seed of the information you want to share, but at the end of the day is not your responsibility what they have chosen to believe. Just mind your own business!

Provide inspiring and healthy feedback. If there seems to be a disconnect, reflect what has been said by paraphrasing. "What I'm hearing is," or "Sounds like you are saying," are great ways to reflect back. Don't simply repeat what the speaker has said verbatim, though; you'll sound insincere or unintelligent. Instead, express what the speaker's words mean to you. Ask questions to clarify certain points: "What do you mean when you say..." or "Is this what you mean?"

"I like to listen. I have learned a great deal from listening carefully. Most people never listen." - Ernest Hemingway

NON-VERBAL COMMUNICATION & BODY LANGUAGE

Nonverbal communication should reinforce what is being said, not contradict it. If you say one thing, but your body language says something else, your listener will likely feel that you're being dishonest. For example, you can't say "yes" while shaking your head no.

If you disagree with or dislike what's being said, you might use negative body language to rebuff the other person's message, such as crossing your arms, avoiding eye contact, or tapping your feet. You don't have to agree with or even like what's being said, but to communicate effectively and not make the other person defensive is important to avoid sending low frequency signals.

Be aware of individual differences as people from different countries and cultures tend to use different nonverbal communication gestures, so it's important to take age, culture, religion, gender, and emotional state into account when reading body language signals. An American teen, a grieving widow, and an Asian businessman, for example, are likely to use nonverbal signals differently.

Look at nonverbal communication signals as a group. Don't read too much into a single gesture or nonverbal cue. Consider all of the nonverbal signals you receive, from eye contact to tone of voice to body language. Anyone can slip up occasionally and let eye contact go, for example, or briefly cross their arms without meaning to. Consider the signals as a whole to get a better "read" on a person.

Use nonverbal signals that match up with your words rather than contradict them. If you say one thing, but your body language says something else, your listener will feel confused or suspect that you're being dishonest. For example, sitting with your arms crossed and shaking your head doesn't match words telling the other person that you agree with what they're saying.

Adjust your nonverbal signals according to the context. The tone of your voice, for example, should be different when you're addressing a child than when you're addressing a group of adults. Similarly, take into account the emotional state and cultural background of the person you're interacting with.

Avoid negative body language and, instead, use body language to convey positive feelings, even when you're not actually experiencing them. If you're nervous about a situation, a job interview, an important presentation, or first date, for example, you can use positive body language to signal confidence, even though you're not feeling it. Instead of tentatively entering a room with your head down, eyes averted and sliding into a chair, try standing tall with your shoulders back, smiling and maintaining eye contact, and delivering a firm handshake. It will make you feel more self-confident and help to put the other person at ease.

Are your hands clenched? Is your breath shallow? Are you "forgetting" to breathe?

Take a moment to calm down before deciding to continue a conversation or postpone it.

The best way to rapidly and reliably relieve stress is through the senses, sight, sound, touch, taste, smell, or movement. For example, you could pop a peppermint in your mouth, squeeze a stress ball in your pocket, take a few deep breaths, clench and relax your muscles, or simply recall a soothing, sensory-rich image. Each person responds differently to sensory input, so you need to find a coping mechanism that is soothing to you.

Look for humor in the situation. When used appropriately, humor is a great way to relieve stress when communicating. When you or those around you start taking things too seriously, find a way to lighten the mood by sharing a joke or an amusing story.

Be willing to compromise. Sometimes, if you can both bend a little, you'll be able to find a happy middle ground that reduces the stress levels for everyone concerned. If you realize that the other person cares much more about an issue than you do, compromise may be easier for you and a good investment for the future of the relationship.

Agree to disagree, if necessary, and take time away from the situation so everyone can calm down. Go for a stroll outside if possible, or spend a few minutes meditating. Physical movement or finding a quiet place to regain your balance can quickly reduce stress.

Direct, assertive expression makes for clear communication and can help boost your self-esteem and decision-making skills. Being assertive means expressing your thoughts, feelings, and needs in an open and honest way, while standing up for yourself and respecting others. It does NOT mean being hostile, aggressive, or demanding. Effective communication is always about understanding the other person, not about winning an argument, or forcing your opinions on others.

INSPIRE OTHER WHEN YOU COMMUNICATE

This is, in my opinion, the most important aspect of communication: inspiring others. It is not telling people what to do in their lives, but planting a seed in their consciousness, with a positive value in order to inspire the listener to believe with the hope that a better life and world is possible. You can influence people and cause even other people to have joyful leaps in their own life. This is when you become a real influencer of the collective consciousness, and I am not talking about Instagram or TikTok; I am talking about how, through communication, we can transform our world.

This is what communicating inspiration is all about; impacting lives through communication. It really requires emotional intelligence to identify the other person's emotional state and how you can inspire them to experience joy, a happy moment, to change their mood or change in their belief system and values. When you do it from your heart, the satisfaction of impacting someone else's life in a positive way is as present as the profound joy and gratitude that you will immediately feel.

You can say it directly or indirectly with your actions and non-verbal communication. You don't necessarily need to say something or be "preachy", just Inspire with your actions, with your life, with everything that comes out of your voice; let it be fertile soil for others. You don't need to put people down with what you say. Lift them up by communicating with others within their value system and inspire them. Access those values that motivate and inspire people to move forward. It can be a friend, a co-worker, an employee, an investor, or a team member.

SOLVING PROBLEMS

If there is a problem or argument that you are involved in, before letting things escalate, be kind and communicate solutions for a "problem". Use linguistics presuppositions.

Negotiate & Create metaphors. Move concepts from the micro to macro, and vice versa. Discover values to solve a dispute or conflict. Find new ways of saying no.

Problem Solver Model

1. What is the problem?
2. What is the Root Cause of the issue?
3. Have I procrastinated to resolve this?
4. How would I like to transform that?
5. When will it stop me from being a limitation?
6. How will I know I have solved the problem?
7. How am I changing and seeing things differently now?
8. How do I know?

ASK YOURSELF:

1. Am I giving my full attention when other people talk to me?
2. When was the last time I finish a conversation that left me feeling happy?
3. What do I communicate with my body when people talk to me? Am I comparing my life to what they are saying, or am I really listening?
4. Where can my communication skills improve?

5. Is there an unnecessary communication habit I learned from my family or community that doesn't really serve me anymore? What is it, and how can you transform it?
6. How will I know that I have improved my communication skills?

PRINCIPLE 58

Effective communication protects your joy.

PRINCIPLE 59

Inspire with your communication.

PRINCIPLE 60

If it is not nice, don't say it.

PRINCIPLE 61

Become a problem solver when you speak.

PRINCIPLE 62

Become an active listener.

EMPATHY

> *Empathy is the ability to step outside of your own bubble and into the bubbles of other people."*
>
> – C. Joybell

EMPATHY IS A word that is often used by many people. It's commonly known that empathy is a good thing to have, but it isn't always a priority in people's lives.

Did you know that 98% of people have the ability to empathize with others? The few exceptions are psychopaths, narcissists, and sociopaths, who are people who are unable to understand or relate to other people's feelings and emotions. Even they can change.

Other groups of people that might struggle to understand other people's emotions are those who are on the Autism Spectrum. However, many people feel that people on the Autism Spectrum are still, although perhaps not in the traditional way.

While a large majority of the population is capable of empathy, sometimes the practice of it is limited or none at all. But what is empathy, and why is it important?

Can empathy be developed, or are we born with a certain amount? Are some people just naturally better at empathizing? Is it really as important as some people say it is to practice empathy?

WHAT IS EMPATHY?

> *The highest form of knowledge is empathy."*
>
> – Bill Bullard

In simple terms, empathy is the ability to understand things from another person's perspective. It's the ability to share someone else's feelings and emotions and understand why they have those feelings. Many famous people have talked about the importance of understanding and empathy.

Maya Angelou once said,

> *I think we all have empathy. We may not have enough courage to display it."*

Albert Einstein said,

> *Peace cannot be kept by force; it can only be achieved by understanding."*

Former President Barack Obama has said,

> *The biggest deficit that we have in our society and in the world right now is an empathy deficit. We are in great need of people being able to stand in somebody else's shoes and see the world through their eyes."*

DIFFERENT TYPES OF EMPATHY

In an attempt to define what empathy is, people have created different categories of empathy. According to psychologists Daniel Goleman and Paul Ekman, there are three types of empathy: cognitive, emotional, and compassionate.

- Cognitive empathy. Cognitive empathy is the ability to understand how someone else feels and to work out what they might be thinking.
- Emotional empathy or Affective empathy. Emotional empathy refers to the ability to share another person's emotions. This would mean when you see someone else who is sad, it then makes you feel sad.
- Compassionate empathy or Empathic Concern. Compassionate empathy is when you turn feelings into actions. It goes beyond

understanding and relating to other people's situations and pushed an individual to do something.

WHY IS EMPATHY IMPORTANT?

Empathy is important in almost every aspect of daily life. It allows us to have compassion for others relate to friends, loved ones, co-workers, and strangers, and it has a large beneficial impact on the world.

Healthy relationships require nurture, care, and understanding. A friendship or romantic relationship that lacks empathy and understanding will soon flounder. When people only think of their own interests, the other people in the relationships will suffer.

If one spouse in a marriage forgoes seeing things from the other's perspective, they will likely have marital issues. No two people are ever going to think exactly alike, and no two people are going to have the same experiences. Both people in a relationship bring their own ideas, life experiences, and struggles. Without taking the time to try to relate to one another's feelings and perspectives, people in relationships will likely feel unloved and uncared for.

For many people, a workplace is a place for teamwork. For things that require a group effort, it's extremely important to take the time to relate to co-workers. Even if people are not specifically working on one project, it is still important to get along with fellow workers. Using empathy is a vital part of a smooth working relationship. Without it, it's much easier to fall into disputes and disagreements.

It is also highly important for management to use empathy. Bosses who lack empathy are likely to subject their employees to unfair practices. Managers who are without empathy may push employees to work beyond what is healthy and reasonable or maybe unduly harsh when an employee makes a mistake.

Higher amounts of empathy in the workplace have been linked to increased performance, increased sales, and better leadership abilities.

Empathy from a global perspective is infinitely important, especially when it leads to compassion. This type of empathy pushes people to dive in and help when there are major disasters. People are willing to help out others that they have never met because they know that they, too, would need help if things were reversed.

Without compassionate empathy, the world would be a much darker and less functional place to live. You can bring so much happiness to your life by just practicing empathy.

Empathy enhances having compassion and can be roughly defined in terms of a state of mind that is nonviolent, non-harming, and nonaggressive. It is a mental attitude based on the wish for others to be free of their suffering and is associated with a sense of commitment, responsibility, and respect towards the other.

ASK YOURSELF:

1. Am I a good listener and observer?
2. When was the last time I did something kind to a stranger?
3. When was the last time I help someone in need?
4. How can I improve my Empathy levels?
5. How will I know I have improved this skill?
6. What kind of situations can I show empathy and will in return fulfill me with Joy and happiness?

PRINCIPLE 63

Practice empathy.

FRIENDSHIP

"A friend is someone who understands your past, believes in your future, and accepts you just the way you are."

– Anonymous

FRIENDSHIPS CAN HAVE a major impact on your happiness, health, and well-being, but it's not always easy to build or maintain friendships. It is important to understand the value of friendships in your life and what you can do to develop and nurture your friendships.

Good friends can bring so much joy to our lives. A good friend can help you celebrate good times and provide support during bad times. Friends prevent loneliness and give you a chance to offer needed companionship, too. Exploring the world and growing with a pal, sharing values and beliefs, but more importantly, sharing the bliss of life. People who live a long life have in common that they have friends, they have strong bonds on the planet that keeps them alive.

Friends can also:

- Increase your sense of belonging and purpose.
- Boost your happiness and reduce your stress.
- Improve your self-confidence and self-worth.
- Help you cope with traumas, such as divorce, serious illness, job loss, or the death of a loved one.
- Encourage you to change or avoid unhealthy lifestyle habits, such as excessive drinking or lack of exercise.

Friends also play a significant role in promoting your overall health. Adults with strong social support have a reduced risk of many significant health problems, including depression, high blood pressure, and an unhealthy body mass index. Studies have even found that older adults with a rich social life are likely to live longer than their peers with fewer connections.

WHY IS IT SOMETIMES HARD TO MAKE FRIEND OR MAINTAIN?

Many adults find it hard to develop new friendships or keep up existing friendships. Friendships may take a back seat to other priorities, such as work or caring for children or aging parents. You and your friends may have grown apart due to changes in your lives or interests. Or maybe you've moved to a new community and haven't found yet a way to meet new people.

Developing and maintaining good friendships takes effort. The enjoyment and comfort friendship can provide, however, makes the investment worthwhile.

Sometimes it is hard to maintain some friendships because of a lack of respect from one side or both sides. It is important that you respect your friendships and only lift their lives instead of humiliating them or using them merely to boost your ego and cope with your loneliness.

People who use their friendships to boost their ego or to cope with their loneliness are most likely to not understand the value of friendships, the value of things, the value of opportunities. We already talked about toxic people, and if you identify a toxic friend is important to distance yourself from that person as it might be interfering with your growth and expansion. That doesn't mean it is your antagonist, or you need to hate him now, no! It just means you are taking your time to grow in a different direction.

A friend can feel like you have known them forever, and maybe you met them one year ago. If you want to make new friends, you have to expose yourself. Get out there, join groups and events. Remember to mark your calendar to spend time with your friends, the ones that love you, respect you, and inspire you as well as who can together with you enjoy the bliss. It's like a garden; you have to water all the plants; if not, they will die. This also holds true for friendships.

WHAT'S A HEALTHY NUMBER OF FRIENDS?

Quality counts more than quantity. While it's good to cultivate a diverse network of friends and acquaintances, you also want to nurture a few truly close friends who will be there for you through thick and thin.

WHAT ARE SOME WAYS TO MEET NEW PEOPLE?

It's possible that you've overlooked potential friends who are already in your social network. Think through people you've interacted with, even very casually, who made a positive impression.

You may find potential friends among people with whom:

- You've worked or taken classes.
- You've been friends in the past, but have since lost touch.
- Have friends in common.
- You've enjoyed chatting with at social gatherings.
- You share family ties.
- You share a passion or interest.
- You meet at a music festival.
- You are in the same event, live video, chatroom.

If anyone stands out in your memory as someone you'd like to know better, reach out. Ask mutual friends or acquaintances to share the person's contact information, or even better, to reintroduce the two of you with a text, a phone call, a social media message, an email, or an in-person visit. Extend an invitation to coffee or lunch, a music or art event, a sports game, a workout, the options are limitless.

To meet new people who might become your friends, you have to go to places where others are gathered. Don't limit yourself to one strategy for meeting people. The broader your efforts, the greater your likelihood of success.

Persistence also matters. Take the initiative rather than waiting for invitations to come your way and keep reaching out. You may need to suggest plans a few times before you can tell if your interest in a new friend is mutual.

For example, try several of these ideas:

- Attend community events and look for groups or clubs that gather around an interest or hobby you share. These groups are often listed in the newspaper or on community bulletin boards. There are also many websites that help you connect with new friends in your neighborhood or city. Do an Instagram search using terms such as your city or neighborhood, join a dating app.
- Volunteer and offer your time or talents at a hospital, place of healing, museum, community center, charitable group, or other organization. You can form strong connections when you work with people who have mutual interests.
- Extend and accept invitations by inviting a friend to join you for yoga. When you're invited to a social gathering, say yes. Contact someone who recently invited you to an activity and return the favor.
- Take up a new interest and take a college or community education course to meet people who have similar interests. Join a class at a local gym, senior center, or community fitness facility.
- Join a tribe or community and take advantage of special activities and get-to-know-you events for new members.
- Take a walk. Grab your kids or pet and head outside. Chat with neighbors who are also out and about or head to a popular park and strike up conversations there.

Above all, stay positive. You may not become friends with everyone you meet, but maintaining a friendly attitude and demeanor can help you improve the relationships in your life and sow the seeds of friendship with new acquaintances.

HOW DOES SOCIAL MEDIA AFFECT FRIENDSHIPS?

Joining a chat group or online community might help you make or maintain connections and relieve loneliness. However, research suggests that the use of social networking sites doesn't necessarily translate to a larger offline network or closer offline relationships with network members. In addition, remember to exercise caution when sharing personal information or arranging an activity with someone you've only met online.

The power of having a friend to share in-person experiences is vastly valuable.

HOW CAN I NURTURE MY FRIENDSHIPS?

Developing and maintaining healthy friendships involves give-and-take. Sometimes you're the one giving support, and other times you're on the receiving end. Letting friends know you care about them and appreciate them can help strengthen your bond. It's as important for you to be a good friend as it is to surround yourself with good friends.

To nurture your friendships:

- Be kind. This most-basic behavior emphasized during childhood remains the core of successful adult relationships. Think of friendship as an emotional bank account. Every act of kindness and every expression of gratitude are deposits into this account, while criticism and negativity draw down the account.
- Listen up, ask what's going on in your friends' lives. Let the other person know you are paying close attention through eye contact, body language, and occasional brief comments such as, "That sounds fun." When friends share details of hard times or difficult experiences, don't judge them, be empathetic, but don't give advice unless your friends ask for it. Say something that inspires them to reconnect with their own authentic self.
- Open up and Build intimacy with your friends by opening up about yourself. Being willing to disclose personal experiences and concerns shows that your friend holds a special place in your life and deepens your connection.
- Show that you can be trusted. Being responsible, reliable, and dependable is key to forming strong friendships. Keep your engagements and arrive on time. Follow through on commitments

189

you've made to your friends. When your friends share confidential information, keep it private.

- Make yourself available. Building a close friendship takes time together. Make an effort to see new friends regularly, and to check in with them in between meet-ups. You may feel awkward the first few times you talk on the phone or get together, but this feeling is likely to pass as you get more comfortable with each other.
- Manage your nerves with mindfulness. You may find yourself imagining the worst of social situations and feel tempted to stay home. Use mindfulness exercises to reshape your thinking. Each time you imagine the worst, pay attention to how often the embarrassing situations you're afraid of actually take place. You may notice that the scenarios you fear usually don't happen.

When embarrassing situations do happen, remind yourself that your feelings will pass, and you can handle them until they do. Yoga and other mind-body relaxation practices also may reduce social anxiety and help you face situations that make you feel nervous. Remember that there will always be compatibility in a relationship with shared values.

Some friendships are based on wealth, power, or position. In these cases, your friendship continues as long as your power, wealth, or position is sustained. Once these grounds are no longer there, then the friendship"

– DL

A true friend connects from positive emotions, a feeling of closeness and support, in which there is a sense of sharing and connectedness.

The factor that sustains a genuine friendship is a feeling of affection, admiration, trust, love, peace, joy and enlightenment. If you lack that, then you won't be able to sustain a genuine friendship. Stand back and reflect on the basis of the relationship that you value and why they are important in your life.

Remember, it's never too late to build new friendships or reconnect with old friends. Investing time in making friends and strengthening your friendships can pay off in better health, a longer life, and a brighter outlook for years to come.

ASK YOURSELF:

1. Who are my friends? Name each of them, and write it down.
2. Why are they in my life? Which gift each of them brings to my life?
3. What gift do I share with their lives?
4. When was the last time I spent time with my friends?
5. What kind of memories do I love creating with my friends?
6. Which emotions do I like to experience when I am with my friends?
7. Are my friends aligned with my values, beliefs, and purpose?
8. Do I even know the purpose of my friends? Have we spoken about this?
9. From 1 to 10, how proactive am I when it comes to cultivating friendships?
10. How can I manage my time so I can nurture more friendships?
11. When was the last time I met new people?
12. When was the last time I made a new friend I met in-person?
13. Are my friends toxic or abusive with me?
14. How will I know my friends are not taking advantage of me or using me to boost their ego?
15. Is your friendship based on mutual respect? What is the foundation of our friendship?

PRINCIPLE 64

Have a long, happy life with friends.

PRINCIPLE 65

Be open to let new people bring joy into your life.

ROMANTIC RELATIONSHIPS

> *Ultimately the bond of all companionship, whether in marriage or in friendship, is conversation."*
>
> – Oscar Wilde

DALAI LAMA WAS such a wise guy. He really achieved superior levels of enlightenment. But he also didn't experience life as the rest of us. For example, he was in celibacy, and he thought that sex and romantic relationships were psychologically and emotionally messy and dangerous. Now, there might be some levels of truth in that, but I believe we can build healthy, strong, long-lasting romantic relationships and lovers that will bring so much joy to our lives.

Experiencing romance or having a real "lover" has got to be one of the most fun, cathartic, energetic, joyful, and peaceful expressions of life in its purest form. It responds to one of the basic biological survival elements of reproduction and companionship. Unfortunately, with all the distractions we have in our busy lives, it seems many couples never find the time to really be lovingly and gently intimate, and that can lead to love's demise.

Romance is about getting closer, intimacy, to be telepathically aligned, aligned in purpose, values, and beliefs, having a whole set of sensorial qualities for each other. There is also a big difference between sex and romance. In most relationships, if you want it to be great, you have to fully engage in the process of working the relationship and having communication. Again, like gardening!

Most people don't try to do anything romantic in their relationship because they simply don't know how. Here's a hint: There are no secrets to romance and intimacy. Most of the time, everything we need to know is right under our noses. Just get your nose closer and do it more gently! Beautifully mindfully present.

In many cases, all it takes is some encouragement to take a risk and a little appreciation for your partner's efforts, even if they fall a little short. Romance, like life, is seldom perfect, but it can be fulfilling no matter how it differs from what you've seen on the silver screen.

What works for you may or may not work for the one you love. Remember, it's a gift of trust when your partner takes the risk of revealing his or her preferences to you. You may be surprised at how easy it is to create more sizzle and less static with a simple gesture or action.

Intimacy and purpose aligned is the foundation of a great romantic or lovers. A relationship built primarily on sexual desire is like a house built on a foundation of ice; as soon as the ice melts, the building collapses.

To raise a family with your partner it is important that everything is on the table and that you bring emotional stability to the family or relationship through communication. All agreements must be respected in order not to break the trust, the transparency, and communication.

The trust is the most delicate aspect of a relationship; even if it's just a friend, when trust is gone, the relationship is over. A relationship without trust is like living without oxygen.

In any relationship, it is important that all the parties give and take something in order for it all to work; it can't be a one-way street. It needs to work both ways.

From an evolution and biological perspective, it's reproducing ourselves and the need to create a family. Exploring the world together and falling in love every day again.

Eros, the drive toward passionate, romantic love, can be seen as this ancient desire for fusion with the other half. It seems to be a universal, unconscious human need. The feeling involves a sensation of merging with the other, of boundaries breaking down, of becoming one with the loved one. Psychologists call this the collapse of ego boundaries. Some feel that this process is rooted in our earliest experience, an unconscious

ASK YOURSELF:

1. Do I love myself? Do I feel I deserve to be loved?
2. Am I ready to share this love with someone else?
3. How will I know that I am ready?
4. When was the last time I was in a romantic relationship with someone?
5. How did I feel at the time?
6. Why did or didn't it work out?
7. Do I fear success in my love-life because I am boycotting my own happiness?
8. Why am I not allowing me to be in a serious romance?
9. Am I enjoying and growing with my partner?

PRINCIPLE 66

Get out and get in love.

THE FAMILY

"Rejoice with your family in the beautiful land of life."
— Albert Einstein

F AMILY COMES FIRST, they say. You may have said and heard these many times in your life. But have you ever pondered upon why so? Your family creates a strong foundation for your emotional as well as your physical well-being. In most cases, it's a family that people go back to after a day's hard work and unwind, rejuvenate, and re-energize themselves. But how does family bring happiness to your life?

Each member of your family is unique, and so are their needs. But a few common practices can help you generally build a strong, happy, and healthy family.

HOW DOES FAMILY BRINGS HAPPINESS?

Sometimes right from the family, we learn the most important values in our lives, but also the toxic patterns at times. Highlighting more our fears and limitations than the expansion and happiness.

Studies have often shown that individuals with positive and supportive people around them growing up have more emotional stability as oppose to individuals without support.

Nowadays, many people alienate themselves from their loved ones as they allow social media addictions to engulf them. But it's crucial to spend time with your family and create joyful memories together, rather for your own sake than theirs. Make sure all of you go out for picnics, vacations, experiences out of the normal, or have some family activity that you do every week, month, or holidays. The least you can do is to have one meal together.

195

Unfortunately, stress has become a part of most people's lives. But having stress is not an ideal state of being. In stressful situations, you can easily lean back on your family for support, apart from practicing other coping techniques. Speak to your family about what bothers you. It can prove to be a good way of venting out your negative emotions. Your family members may not only hear you out but also provide practical solutions to what is bothering you.

Family can also help you deal with stress by encouraging you to relax your mind through meditation or other such activities. Watching a humorous movie or play with your loved ones can kick stress out of your life. Remember, laughter is the best medicine, and your family can give you many reasons for laughing, having fun, and being happy and joyful.

In all areas of life, be it professionally, personally, or academically setting targets that are achievable and realistic is key. It is good to have a high aim. But having a realistic and practical strategy is equally important to help you chase your dreams. Your family can give you a healthy reality-check when you most need it. It is your family who will not think twice before bringing you back to the ground when you are behaving high headed. Only your near ones can do it in a loving way that doesn't bruise your self-respect but points out where you are lacking. What's more, they are always up for helping you cover up for what is missing.

So, if you are struggling with any aspect of your life, speak to your family members. There is nothing wrong with seeking help from your loved ones. And there's no need to feel ashamed of your wrongdoings either. You can rely on them to help you stay on a good path, and if you should ever go astray, they are the ones to help you come back on track. So, keep your family close and spend time with them.

ASK YOURSELF:

1. How are my relationships with my family?
2. Is there anything I have to forgive my family for?
3. Is there anything I need to be grateful for because of my family?
4. Does family bring me happiness?

5. Does my family accentuate my fears and failures or inspire me to be a better person?
6. Who in my family does bring me happiness? Why?
7. What is the greatest blessing I have received through my family?
8. What advice will I give to myself for the well-being of my family?

PRINCIPLE 67

Family is a stone to lay on and explore the bliss.

THE TRIBE

BUILDING YOUR TRIBE is easier than you think of. Say "yes" to invitations. Recognize that each invitation is an opening, seeking to include you in the divine design of life. For this reason, the likelihood that you will encounter soul connections by showing up every time life invites you out into the community is high. Say "yes" especially when you really want to say "no."

Help others with the same care you do for yourself. Operate from the perspective: What can I give? The getting is in the giving. Hold the door for a stranger, ask to give directions to someone who is lost, and look for ways to serve today. Most importantly, give what you most wish to receive. It can help to write this down in a journal first, then think of ways you can offer it to others.

Go direct into the community by choosing one that is already organized around something that turns you on. Recognize that groups that have already self-organized are "homes" waiting for you. Make yourself an insider by acting as if you belong. Assume your place is waiting for you. Choose a group today and reach out to organize a plan to participate as a member.

Ask yourself, what is my greatest emotional wound? Then organize yourself today to go serve it. If this doesn't immediately spring to mind, spend some time journaling about it. What is the thing that stands most between you and a sense of connection to others? Is it the neglect you suffered as a child? Is it stress from an unhealthy intimate relationship? Go and volunteer at Big Brothers Big Sisters, the women's shelter, etc. Use the thing that severed your connection to trusting life and people to re-establish one.

Walkabout, and look at who and what has been pushed to the edges of your world and go on an adventure into those borders. To go on a modern walkabout, first ask: Who is invisible in my world? Are there children in your life? The elderly? What about people who aren't your color, race, age, gender, or political persuasion?

Make plans today to step outside your comfort zone, and head out into the unknown, not as a tourist (observing for the purposes of entertainment), but as a vulnerable observer; allow yourself to be "remade" by the encounter.

THE COMMUNITY

" It takes a village."

– Anonymous

PUBLIC EFFORTS AROUND happiness. The government of the Himalayan country of Bhutan seems to think so. In particular, Bhutan surveys its citizens in nine key aspects of happiness:

- Psychological well-being
- Physical health
- Time or work-life balance
- Social vitality and connection
- Education
- Arts and culture
- Environment and nature
- Good government
- Material well-being

The use of a "gross national happiness" index has been a policy of Bhutan now for nearly four decades.

As a result of a more recent initiative, the government of Victoria, British Columbia, has been participating in a Happiness Index Partnership comprising the Victoria Foundation, United Way, the University of Victoria, and several local and provincial government agencies to undertake a well-being survey.

A community is defined as a group of people who interact with one another and share common characteristics. Within these communities, people develop strong relationships, from romantic relationships to friendships, anywhere in between, that heavily influence an individual's personal attributes.

Communities are everywhere! There are work communities, cultural, school, political, religious, sports, and other communities that exist all around us. How important are these groups to the mental stability of the average person? An immeasurable important aspect of coexisting. With access to more data collected from research, we are able to understand that a person's overall health is not only determined by their physical well-being, but also how well their mind is doing, the body and mind are linked together, and sometimes one can impact the other.

One of the first, and arguably the most important, communities an individual is exposed to and belongs to is their family community. The significance of good parenting and a person's socioeconomic status plays a huge role in the development of a child's personality and in society.

Children learn a lot of mimicking the speech and actions of their parents and closed people to their social circle, along with the way their parent disciplines and rewards them. For example, if a parent uses swear words often, then the child may pick up the same derogatory words their parents use in public.

Another example is if a parent continuously lies to their child, that specific kid may develop strong trust issues with the whole world since they do not know how to successfully develop and maintain and trustful bond with another person.

A creative or hobby community can bring so much happiness to your life, whether it is a dance community, a choir, a painting community, bingo, surfing, athletic, yoga community, or any fun activity with a group that practices it.

A work community can have a couple of members or an endless amount. Not everyone is going to get along with one another in the workplace, but generally, people who are satisfied with their leaders and co-workers have a better chance of mental peace.

People who are psychologically overwhelmed with the members of their work community will have more stress and less motivation to go to work. If you ever feel defeated in the workplace because of another co-worker, just remember that nobody is perfect. Who are they to make you feel anything but happy?

Another community example is our online community. Technology plays a huge role in communication nowadays. People have developed an online presence and share this community with other peers.

Unfortunately, there has been an uproar that social media has sparked higher levels of anxiety and depression amongst the current generation. Social media is a place of communication via comments, likes, shares, posts, etc. People who work towards endlessly impressing members of their social media community versus positively reinforcing themselves will be less mentally stable.

A tip for success is to remember that happiness is a choice and comes from within, not always from the acceptance of others.

A sense of security, support, love, and acknowledgment help to give us a feeling of purpose and mental safety and stability. As important as it is for a person to love themselves, it is equally important to feel loved and wanted by others. Human connections and communities allow humans to relate and learn from one another in order to understand what it takes to be mentally healthy.

PAYING BACK TO THE COMMUNITY, POLITICS & TAXES

Part of being in a community is contributing to it. Whether you pay back as a volunteer or taking care of the community in other ways, the other way you literally can pay back to the community is by paying your taxes. Take care of your taxes if you live in a country that you need to pay taxes. Make sure all of your numbers are updated, be aware of how much you are financially contributing to the system, that is also giving back to you.

It is very important to care about politics because you should know what is going on around you regarding the well-being of your community. Also, it is important to have a say in what is going on around you. The political decisions people make will affect many lives and your community directly. Many people see politics as the government and the laws being made, and that is true, but it is way more complicated than that. Every law that is made will impact many. Sometimes the decisions will affect people in a bad way and sometimes affect the community in a good way. Every vote that you make will either break people or make people, and therefore it is important to vote and have a voice in your community.

For example, if a new law is made in your area, you might want to make sure that you and the people around you know that a new law has been made so that no one breaks the law without even knowing it. Also, if something dangerous is happening around you or someone you know, you want to be aware if someone is breaking the law. It is very important to know what is happening around you. Everyone should have a say in what will happen, because we all live side by side with each other, and it would not be fair if someone was left out. Also, each vote makes a difference in the ways that we live. It is always important to share your opinion. The way you vote will affect many people and their everyday life.

IF YOU FEEL UNHAPPY WITH THE LAWS OF YOUR COMMUNITY TAKE A MORE ACTIVE ROLE IN POLITICS

You should care about politics in your community because the decisions people make will affect many lives. For example, if someone wanted to build on the land, it might be good for the people who worked in the area, but residents who lived nearby and loved the land and relied on the land for water and food might be devastated. Sometimes things that sound like good ideas might be very devastating later.

These are just a few reasons why you should care about politics. Politics are very important and very complicated. Some people might not care about politics, but they will regret not voting when something bad happens.

Respecting the laws and order of your community will bring so much happiness in your life as it will save you trouble and give you time to focus on the things that bring joy to your life.

If you are unhappy with your current political system, you might want to consider new ways of impacting positively the public opinion regarding whatever is bothering you about the current state of your country. If you feel inspired enough, you might want to consider a career in politics.

MONEY IS ENERGY

We exchange value with our community, and other communities, with the use of money or a currency. Money is energy, not just a material object. Money became a universal way of exchanging value. Can you buy happiness? Yes, but it will wear out. Can you buy joy? Yes, but you have to be wise in the experiences that you are "buying" for yourself because not all of them will bring you joy.

For example, a trip to Las Vegas could buy you happy moments that you will probably forget the next day. On the other hand, an organized trip to visit The Amazonian jungle in Peru, for example, getting to meet tribes, experiencing, and learning from different communities can bring long-lasting joy to your life through perspective thinking. Can you be happy without money? Absolutely! You can create experiences for yourself that will bring joy to your life. Remember, your happiness and joy need to be unconditional for it to really exist freely. The wise you get in life, the sooner you will understand that happiness and joy should not depend on anything, not even in financial wealth.

A SUSTAINABLE COMMUNITY

Every day we go through so much junk and footprint we leave behind us. From what you consume, to what you eat, wear, buy, and even your household temperature leaves a footprint on the planet.

We are in a climate crisis that we are partially responsible for. Most of our trash ends up in the oceans or landfills. Every day that trash and plastic that is polluting our oceans has a negative impact on every ecological environment it touches.

Our energy is not clean; our waters are poisoned and are killing the life within. Our meaty meals produce so much gas emissions, our meals are so filled with chemicals and harmful toxins for our bodies.

It feels like some people care and are aware of this information, but some people are simply too comfortable in their consumption patterns that they can't see the other side of the coin. When you have a world facing an ecological crisis that could lead to a mass extinction it is important that we take actions in our daily lives. From the simplest things like what you buy for food and how you do it, to more complex things like a fully sustainable electricity, water ,or household.

It is selfish and even "narcissistic", ignoring that our irresponsible and unhealthy consumption habits are affecting our coral reefs, our forests, our oceans, our health, and the overall well-being of our planet negatively.

Caring about our planet and contributing from your own household to the sustainable levels of our community is the highest form of love you can show to your community. Even if you start by focusing on having a more sustainable diet, shopping habits.

ASK YOURSELF:

1. How would I describe my role with my community?
2. When was the last time I felt part of a community?
3. Are all the aspects of being integrated into a community active?
4. How can I be more integrated into my community?
5. How can I bring happiness to my communities?
6. Have I found my tribe?
7. How do I make an effort to connect with my tribe?
8. How can I create the space to build my own tribe?
9. When was the last time I was exposed to a tribe that welcomed me?
10. How will I know I am part of a tribe and community?
11. How will I describe my sustainability practices?
12. How much trash and pollution do I produce in one day?
13. How can I improve my sustainability practices?

PRINCIPLE 68

Community is important for happiness.

PRINCIPLE 69

Focus on unconditional happiness

PRINCIPLE 70

Living in harmony with the laws will protect your happiness.

THE EARTH, THE SUN, THE UNIVERSE

Not only are we in the Universe, the Universe is in us. I don't know of any deeper spiritual feeling than what that brings upon me."

– Neil deGrasse Tyson

THERE'S SOMETHING ABOUT connecting with the Earth that harmonizes our internal rhythms, induces inner-peace, and recharges us.

Personally speaking, throughout the challenges of life, it seems to me that it is Mother Earth and a profound connection with nature that, above all else, that has been my greatest healing and joy.

MOTHER EARTH INDUCES HEALING, EXPANSION, AND JOY

Mother Earth is an electromagnetic being, and so are we! We are made of the same stuff. Not surprisingly, when we connect with nature, our energetic frequency begins to oscillate the same frequency as the Earth. We attune to her heartbeat, her breath, and she holds us. Our moods and emotions change.

Our modern world has encouraged us to become increasingly disconnected from nature. We live indoors, wear shoes that create a barrier to the Earth, work in offices, are subject to constant distraction, hyper-stimulation, and generally, there is a lack of connection with nature.

In our 'modern' world, we pick up frequencies that are not us, electromagnetic frequencies (EMF) from the swathes of gadgets and appliances that surround us.

In essence, we are constantly taking on frequencies that aren't very supportive of our minds and human bodies, frequencies that conflict with our natural resonance.

Without being connected to the Earth, we become unearthed. Without grounding, it becomes difficult for us to discharge the frequencies that we've taken on board. We become overwhelmed and washed through with chaotic energies.

When I say energies, I also mean negative energies/projections from others, energies from the 'go-go-go' hyper-stimulation of the modern world, unnatural things, and other challenging situations.

This stress on our system creates stress and anxiety. Over time, it takes its toll on our mental and physical health too. Without a connection with the Earth, we don't get that incredible sense of supportive calm and well-being that happens naturally when we are earthed.

Connecting with the Earth literally brings us to life. It breathes us. It restores and rejuvenates our energy field. The frequency of Mother Earth is incredibly healing. It's perfectly configured for optimal human beingness.

Connecting with the Earth:

- It is an instant way to discharge unwanted energies mentally, physically, and emotionally; it grounds us.
- Restores and rejuvenates our energy field.
- Promotes an instant sense of calm.
- Improves mental and emotional clarity.
- Helps to get in touch with our true selves.
- Can ease depression and anxiety.

The mental and emotional well-being associated with connecting with the Earth can have a positive knock-on effect to other challenges in our lives, including physical, disease and illness.

PLANTS

While mental health experts warn about depression as a global epidemic, other researchers are discovering ways we trigger our natural production of happy chemicals that keep depression at bay, with surprising results. All you need to do is get your fingers dirty and harvest your own food.

In recent years I've come across two completely independent bits of research that identified key environmental triggers for two important chemicals that boost our immune system and keep us happy, serotonin and dopamine.

Getting your hands dirty in the garden can increase your serotonin levels. Serotonin is a happy chemical, a natural anti-depressant, and strengthens the immune system. Lack of serotonin in the brain causes depression.

Another interesting bit of research relates to the release of dopamine in the brain when we harvest products from the garden. The researchers hypothesize that this response evolved over nearly 200,000 years of hunter gathering, that when food was found (gathered or hunted), a flush of dopamine released in the reward center of the brain triggered a state of bliss or mild euphoria. The dopamine release can be triggered by sight (seeing a fruit or berry) and smell as well as by the action of actually plucking the fruit.

Besides the experience of gardening, plants can also be ingested. Elevating your diet to a plant-based diet will have so many positive repercussions in your body-mind-spirit, and what I mean is in your joy.

Plants are medicine like Hippocrates said. You can also use plants as a tool for your joy and enlightenment. For example, psychedelic plants are a great tool to have when it comes to healing the mind-body-spirit. Be mindful and respectful in the way you inject them, but know that they are a unique tool that can bring healing to your life. That is the approach you should always have when it comes to psychedelics.

ANIMALS & PETS

As crazy as it may sound, interacting with animals has the capability to reduce stress in humans bring joy to our lives. Among most animals on the planet, dogs have been conditioned to work and respond well to human behavior and emotion. In addition to their ability to comprehend words humans use with them, they are experts in making sense of our tone, particularly when trying to discipline or address something, physical body language, and connecting on an emotional level where they are able to interpret how we are feeling.

Humans usually invest in pets for the pure sense of joy and companionship; however, it has been proven that owning a dog can beneficially contribute to an owner's physical and mental health. Science has there is a strong emotional connection and exertion of feelings between humans and pets.

THE SUN

Happiness, Health, and Light. The correlation of light and mood is dependent on the body's natural response mechanisms to produce serotonin, a neurotransmitter that helps to elevate the mood; and melatonin, a hormone that promotes sleep. When the body recognizes sunlight through the optic nerve, the gland in the brain, which regulates melatonin slows its function, and serotonin levels increase. When light is diminished, the body increases the secretion of melatonin, and the secretion of serotonin is conversely slowed.

Being out in the sun is proven to make you healthier, not just emotionally, but physically as well. It promotes healthier attitudes toward diet and exercise and gives us our dose of Vitamin D, which can be hard to get from foods alone. Vitamin D promotes healthy cell and bone growth, reduces inflammation, and helps to stimulate immune function. Being exposed to the sun can lower blood pressure, create stronger bones and teeth, reduce the risk of breast and colon cancer, and can help to cure skin conditions, including psoriasis and eczema. But don't forget to protect your skin with sunscreen when you're soaking up those rays!

Being in the sun also increases our vitality and energy. Richard Ryan, a psychology professor at the University of Rochester, states that "research has shown that people with a greater sense of vitality don't just have more energy for things they want to do, they are also more resilient to physical illnesses. One of the pathways to health may be to spend more time in natural settings."

Just getting outside can do wonders for our health. Living in the developed modern world, it can be easy to forget our natural cycles and our most innate needs. We have synthetic lights, so we do not necessarily need to follow nature's clock. Yet being in the presence of nature is so essential. It is inextricable from our being, and once we acknowledge this, there is bliss.

EXTRATERRESTRIAL LIFE REPRESENTS EXPANSION

We are not alone in the universe. A few years ago, this notion seemed farfetched; today, the existence of extraterrestrial intelligence is taken for granted by most scientists. Even the staid National Academy of Sciences has gone on record that contact with other civilizations "is no longer something beyond our dreams but a natural event in the history of mankind that will perhaps occur in the lifetime of many of us." Sir Bernard Lovell, one of the world's leading radio astronomers, has calculated that even allowing for a margin of error of 5000%, there must be in our galaxy about 100 million stars which have planets of the right chemistry, dimensions, and temperature to support organic evolution.

If we consider that our own galaxy, the Milky Way, is but one of at least a billion other galaxies similar to ours in the observable universe, the number of stars that could support some form of life is, to reach for a word, astronomical. As to advanced forms of life-advanced by our own miserable earth standards-Dr. Frank D. Drake of the National Radio Astronomy Observatory at Green Bank, West Virginia, has stated that putting all our knowledge together, the number of civilizations which could have arisen by now is about one billion. The next question is, where *is* everybody?

Sooner or later, we will start to publicly incorporate extraterrestrial life in our culture and lifestyle, and when that happens, we need to assimilate it and understand that the information we will receive from extraterrestrial life not only will contribute to our evolution and understanding of our planet, our values, and beliefs, but will also contribute to our new quantum joyfulness.

ASK YOURSELF:

1. How often do I connect with Mother Earth?
2. When was the last time I felt integrated into nature?
3. How often do I connect with plants?
4. How often do I connect with the wild and animal life?
5. How will I know I am ready for extraterrestrial life?

PRINCIPLE 71

Nature nurtures you with life, joy, peace, and enlightenment.

PRINCIPLE 72

Gardening will bring you joy.

PRINCIPLE 73

Connect with the animal kingdom.

PRINCIPLE 74

Expansion takes you to new levels of happiness.

PART VI

TRAINING FOR HAPPINESS

HAPPINESS IS A MUSCLE THAT NEEDS TO BE DEVELOPED

"The mere sense of living is joy enough."
— Emily Dickinson

BEING HAPPY IS like a muscle we need to develop and exercise. When I say "training" the body-spirit and mind, in this context, I'm not referring to "mind" merely as one's cognitive ability or intellect. Rather, I'm using the term in the sense of the Tibetan word Sem, which has a much broader meaning, closer to psyche or spirit. It includes body, intellect and feeling, heart, and mind.

By bringing about a certain inner discipline, we can undergo a transformation of our attitude, our entire outlook, and approach to living.

SELF-DISCIPLINE

"The first and the best victory is to conquer self."
— Plato

Self-discipline is the ability to do what you should be doing, whatever that is. Self-discipline often means putting off your immediate comfort or wishes in favor of long-term success. For example, if you want to become physically fit, you might endure the short-term discomfort of 5:00 a.m. gym times to attain the long-term benefits of being healthy and feeling great.

Self-discipline, like everything else, is a practice. Not every day will be perfect, but each day with its failures and small wins is progress, and that's what self-discipline is all about.

> *Willpower is what separates us from the animals. It's the capacity to restrain our impulses, resist temptation — do what's right and good for us in the long run, not what we want to do right now. It's central, in fact, to civilization."*
>
> – Dr. Roy Baumeister, Ph.D.

> *The State which we have founded must possess the four cardinal virtues of wisdom, courage, discipline and justice … Justice is the principle which has in fact been followed throughout, the principle of one man one job, of minding one's own business, in the sense of doing the job for which one is naturally fitted and not interfering with other people."*
>
> – Plato

Stoicism is an ancient Greco-Roman philosophy. The ideal for the Stoic, as with the Buddhist, is to show complete equanimity in the face of adversity.

The four virtues of Stoicism are wisdom, justice, courage, and temperance. Temperance is subdivided into self-control, discipline, and modesty.

I think when you practice self-discipline, everything else falls into place. Discipline is the fundamental action, mindset, and philosophy, which keeps one in a routine and making progress towards whatever one is pursuing. Stoicism cultivates iron will in anyone who adheres to its teachings. Here are four lessons I've taken away, which have helped me develop discipline in regard to my health and overall quality of life.

KNOW YOUR WEAKNESS

We all have weaknesses. Whether they're snacks such as potato chips or chocolate chip cookies, or technology such as Facebook or the latest addictive game app, they have similar effects on us.

REMOVE TEMPTATIONS

Like the saying goes, "out of sight, out of mind." It may seem silly, but this phrase offers powerful advice. By simply removing your biggest temptations from your environment, you will greatly improve your self-discipline.

SET CLEAR GOALS AND EXECUTION PLANS

If you hope to achieve self-discipline, you must have a clear vision of what you hope to accomplish. If you are trying to accomplish developing your "happiness filter" or your "happy glasses" it is important you outline exactly what you want to achieve within that happiness. You must also have an understanding of what success means to you. After all, if you don't know where you are going, it's easy to lose your way or get side-tracked.

Setting specific, measurable goals is also key to staying motivated. Plan ahead and make your physical activity, your spiritual activity, your mindful activity, or your goal a priority. Stay focused, and prioritize your goals over something else. Visualize your outcome.

A clear plan outlines each step you must take in order to reach your goals. Figure out who you are and what you are about. Create a mantra to keep yourself focused. Successful people use this technique to stay on track and establish a clear finish line. In my experience, working with mantras really helped me not only to start my day in the right direction but also to experience positive thoughts and happiness early in my day.

Practice, fail, start over. Seek instant gratification and reward yourself. As important as the long-term health benefits of exercise are, simply being aware of them isn't enough to motivate most people. Instead, research suggests you should focus on the more immediate benefits.

The key is identifying what the short-term payoff of exercise is for you. Is it sounder sleep? A better mood? Clearer thinking? Less pain? More patience?

Give yourself something to be excited about by planning a reward when you accomplish your goals. Just like when you were a little kid and got a treat for good behavior, having something to look forward to gives you the motivation to succeed.

Anticipation is powerful, and it gives you something to obsess over and focus on, so you're not only thinking of what you are trying to change, you are doing. And when you achieve your goal, find a new goal and a new reward to keep yourself moving forward.

We aren't born with self-discipline; it's a learned behavior. And just like any other skill you want to master, it requires daily practice and repetition. Just like going to the gym, willpower and self-discipline take a lot of work. The effort and focus that self-discipline requires can be draining.

As time passes, it can become more and more difficult to keep your willpower in check. The bigger the temptation or decision, the more challenging it can feel about tackling other tasks that also require self-control. So work on building your self-discipline through daily diligence.

MORAL DISCIPLINE

Similarly, the determination to refrain from lying, divisive speech, hurtful speech, idle gossip, covetousness, malice, and holding wrong views is also moral discipline.

In Buddhist countries, moral discipline is regarded as very important, and it is for this reason that monks and nuns are held in such high esteem. However, it is not only monks and nuns who need to practice moral discipline; everyone needs to practice moral discipline because it is the root of all future happiness.

CONSCIOUS DISCIPLINE: RITUALS

In my experience, I was able to develop my self-discipline by developing healthy rituals. Rituals help us create a culture of connection with our actions. Caring with a willingness to engage, cooperate, and problem solve challenges in our everyday life. A ritual is about doing something with an intention in order to impact your life or manifest something.

Create a ritual for your mornings. It might sound radical, but if you think about it, you will find that you already practice some rituals in your life like brushing your teeth before bed, calming your hair, daily hygiene practices, among other activities you already practice. Guess what? They might already be rituals you have already developed, and unconsciously they might be cultivating your discipline. Create a morning ritual and before bed rituals.

Create rituals when you wake up. Example:

- Morning hygiene practices.
- Yoga – workout, physical activity. Morning meditation – gratefulness, setting an intention for the day.
- Nourishment intake, coffee, breakfast.

Example of rituals before bed are:

- Nighttime hygiene practices.
- Write in my daily journal.
- Skin hydration.
- Nighttime meditation.

Having daily rituals will help you to be aware of your disciplinary practices and will strengthen your discipline. It will give you right away in the morning an immediate reward and a sense of accomplishment. Even drinking coffee can become your morning ritual. You don't need to have three things; you can have more or less. The important thing is to have even one because sooner or later, you will find that you are disciplined with cultivating joy in your life by creating time for the things you love and that make you happy and joyful.

ORGANIZATION AND TIME MANAGEMENT

When you organize, you can literally do anything you set your mind into. You will find out that time is not linear, that you can stretch time and use it in your favor to do all the things you have to do. People often say things like, "I could never do that because I don't have time to do so", and that is because they are yet to develop self-discipline and time management. A good small tip you can take with you about time management is, get a calendar and try to organize your days for a month in advance. Set notifications to remind you of what you have to do and check your calendar often.

A to-do list will also help you to achieve the things that you have per day in your calendar, and it will keep you on track on what's next. I have a to-do list for every day I work, it is a very key tool in my daily life.

That doesn't mean you will be living a rigid life that is all structured at all, there is always time to change plans, and you should always be open for spontaneity to knock at your door. But basing your days in spontaneity will never get you to develop self-discipline skills to achieve your goals and joyful leaps goals.

In the following and last part of the book, you will find what the 22 days transformation program is all about in a more detailed way. However, it requires self-discipline, body-mind-spirit connection to live a joyful and happy life in which you are manifesting and creating an opportunity for yourself.

ASK YOURSELF:

1. From 1 to 10, how disciplined am I?
2. How can I improve my discipline skills?
3. Which rituals can I adopt in the morning and at night to set an intention to my day and plans?
4. How will I know I am a self-disciplined person?

PRINCIPLE 75

Being proactive with your happiness requires self-discipline.

PRINCIPLE 76

Create morning rituals.

MANTRAS

> *You are a cosmic flower. Om chanting is the process of opening the psychic petals of that flower."*
>
> – Amit Ray

MANTRAS HAVE BEEN around for at least 3,000 years. They are not necessarily associated with any religion, even though some religions use mantras in their practices. Mantras are having a mainstream moment now, and that's awesome! We meditate on them. We find them in music that encourages us to "Let It Go" and get "Happy". We tape them to our fridges and computers, pin them to our Pinterest boards, a TikTok dance, InstaQuote them on Instagram.

In a contemplative context, a mantra is a word, sound, or invocation used to aid concentration for meditation or to create intention and purpose in your actions. Your mantra becomes the intention of the day, of the moment, of the movement. It gives you an immediate sense of direction, vision, and purpose.

> Whatever it is that you may be looking to create in your life, state it in the present tense as if it's happening now: 'I am healthy'; 'I am strong'; 'I am open to receiving abundance in all forms.' Notice when you say the mantra out loud: Does it feel light? Does it ground you and make you feel good? If yes, then there it is! Then the practice comes by reminding yourself throughout the day to breathe, speak, and live the mantra out loud and stay open to life, bringing you exactly what you are asking for."
>
> – Rachelle Tratt, Venice, California;
> founder, The Neshama Project

Now, in order to create the Joyful Leap with mantras, in the quantum, you have to say it in the present. As if you already have that quality or value. Each person can find and create their own mantra. Here are a few examples:

For Strength and Willpower,

"FORWARD PROGRESS JUST KEEP MOVING"

For Enduring Tough Times,

"YOU ARE THE SKY EVERYTHING ELSE IS JUST THE WEATHER"

For Manifesting Love,

"I AM ALWAYS ATTRACTING ALL THE LOVE I DREAM OF AND DESERVE"

For Neutralizing Body-Image Issues,

"I AM STRONG, I AM BEAUTIFUL, I AM ENOUGH"

For Radiating Gratitude,

"I AM GRATEFUL FOR ALL THAT IS UNFOLDING IN MY LIFE"

For Starting the Day,

"I MAKE JOYFUL LEAPS EVERY DAY"

"I AM THE BLISS"

"I WEAR MY HAPPY GLASSES WHEN CHALLENGES ARISE"

"I AM FREE BECAUSE MY JOY IS UNCONDITIONAL"

"I AM FULFILLED, I AM FEARLESS"

"I AM FULFILLED, FEARLESS AND STRONG"

"I AM BEAUTIFUL, AND I AM LOVED."

At the end of the day,

"ITS SAFE FOR ME TO FALL ASLEEP, AND REST MY BODY AND CONNECT TO THE UNCONSCIOUS-ENERGY OF THE UNIVERSE"

"THINGS ARE ALWAYS WORKING OUT IN MY FAVOR"

"I AM HEALING EVERY DAY"

"MY CELLS REGENERATE, MY IMMUNE SYSTEM REGENERATES AND MY DNA CHANGES EVERY TIME I MAKE A JOYFUL LEAP"

"I RELEASE ANY EMOTIONAL ATTACHMENT FROM THE DAY AND REPLACE IT WITH PEACE"

Others,

"I AM GRATEFUL FOR EVERY CELL AND ATOMS OF MY BODY"

"MOVING FORWARD, RAISING HIGHER, ATTRACTING ALWAYS THE LOVE I DESERVE TO ACQUIRE"

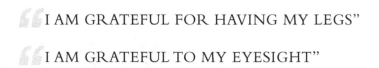

"I AM GRATEFUL FOR HAVING MY LEGS"

"I AM GRATEFUL TO MY EYESIGHT"

OM

Pronunciation: A-U-M

OM is said to be the first sound heard at the creation of the universe. When each syllable is pronounced fully, you should feel the energy of the sound lifting from your pelvic floor up through your head's crown. The Om's droning sound is said to unblock the throat chakra, which can lead to more attuned communication with others.

You can practice your mantras all day at any time, but if you include them in your morning or/and nightly rituals, it will have a very strong impact on your day and experience.

ASK YOURSELF:

1. Have I been unconsciously practicing a mantra without knowing?
2. How would a playlist of positive songs or "mantras" sound?
3. What is the main issue I need to heal, work, or address in my life?
4. Which mantras are a good start for my life at this moment?
5. How many mantras can I create for myself to incorporate into my life?
6. In which moments should I practice specific mantras?

PRINCIPLE 77

Adopt mantras into your life.

JOYFUL PRACTICES

KEEP A DAILY JOURNAL

Practicing evening retrospections on a consistent basis will allow you to become more self-aware through every step of your day because you will be actively gathering information to formulate and articulate constructive answers to the latter questions even when you finish this "class" or "program.

ASK YOURSELF EVERY DAY:

1. What did I do well today?
2. Where were my discipline and self-control tested, where did I do good?
3. When was I grateful?
4. Did I help someone or do a random act of kindness?
5. What did I do that was low? Why did this occur?
6. Did I filter my actions before I acted? Or I simply automatically responded from my first emotions?
7. Furthermore, how can I improve?

PRINCIPLE 78

Document your path towards happiness in a journal.

TREAT YOURSELF

Go to a spa and get a massage. Treat yourself! Buy yourself something special. Get a self-massage. If you enjoy a massage, here's one more reason to get one: massage can boost all 4 of your happy hormones.

According to 2004 research published in International Journal of Neuroscience, both serotonin and dopamine levels increased after a massage. Massage is also known to boost endorphins (Trusted Source and Oxytocin Trusted Source). You can get these benefits from a massage by a licensed massage therapist, but you can also get a massage from a partner for some extra oxytocin. Get one! Ask your lover to massage you, or a friend, a family member, or simply book one now!

Take yourself to a very special dinner with yourself. Buy yourself a special gift, something that will make you happy! Do a facial, practice self-pleasure, cook a very healthy and fancy meal for you. Listen to your favorite mood booster playlist. Get yourself an epic vacation plan. Eat that dark chocolate in the middle of the night if you want.

PRINCIPLE 79

Treat Yourself.

ENJOY LIFE BLAMELESSLY

When we're stuck in resentment, self-condemnation, or guilt, our capacity for joy is severely limited. Everyone makes mistakes, so it's important that we learn how to let go of blame, for others and for ourselves.

Resentment consumes energy, even when we're entitled to it. You obviously want to use your energy to feel the bliss. If you're trying to let go of blame toward someone else, try becoming curious about a hurtful experience, instead of taking it personally. Taking a more impersonal view of disappointments can reveal their hidden gifts. When you're trying to break the habit of self-recriminating thought, focus instead on how you WANT to feel. Always focus on how you want to feel! Rather than dwelling on a mistake, recall the pleasant feeling you have when you choose wisely or accomplish something successfully, and let that feeling be your guide to make a joyful leap and even transform that situation.

It can take several months for neural circuits to consolidate fully in support of new habits of mind, so be vigilant. You are wiring your brain to fully experience JOY AND HAPPINESS instead of just relief at avoiding error.

PRINCIPLE 80

Be Blameless.

HELP OTHERS

When you are happy and want to share that happiness with others, you can do it by sharing something that makes us happy as a whole. You can share it by inspiring them to be happy by simply appreciating nature together. You will find happiness by making other people happy.

Sometimes other people will ask for your help, answer the phone, the text, the DM's. Help them!

Even if you are just buying a meal for the homeless or volunteering in your community, be useful for someone else, and you will feel so much joy! I guarantee it!

PRINCIPLE 81

Help others without expecting anything in return.

HAVE A SENSE OF HUMOR

The humor of someone comes from that space or emotion they hold the most or have held at some point. A happy humor is the humor of the now, the things in front of you, the irony of the moment, the physical comedy of clumsiness, the unusual of each present. Make sure you're not bullying, or your sense of humor is at the expense of someone else's sufferings.

Here are some basic ways you can improve your sense of humor:

- Try to see the funny side of almost everything.
- Learn some jokes!
- Hang out with funny people.
- Stay positive.

PRINCIPLE 82

Have some humor.

BE PRESENT

Get off your phone and pay attention to what's in front of you and your surroundings.

Be a witness, an observer by becoming aware of what you are doing, exactly what you are doing in any given moment, bear witness to it. Observe it, name it, and stand away from it. The moment is now! When we cling to a "now", rather than simply bearing witness to it and letting it pass by, we become trapped in time as it passes.

The art of the present moment is how you can optimize each present to be more joyful and happy, pushing the best outcome of each moment.

PRINCIPLE 83

Be present.

NOTICE THE BEAUTY AROUND YOU AND IN YOU

Noticing the beauty, and focusing on the beauty helps us adjust the lens in which we perceive the world. Sharing beautiful things with a person virtually sets us in the right mood. Beautify and healthily yourself.

Try these three ways:

1. Build Wonder

   Look for beauty in the little things. Anyone can marvel at a striking sunset or a stunning mountain landscape, but challenge yourself to appreciate the beauty in the little things: One leaf, swaying back and forth as it falls from a tree; the light that fills a person's eyes as they begin to smile; two people talking and connecting at a bus stop as you drive by. As we begin to appreciate these little things, we realize that life is a collection of tiny moments. We can see and experience them, or we can miss them.

2. Build Awe and Admiration

   Place yourself in environments where you're most likely to be filled with awe and admiration. For example, spend time regularly in nature, in art museums, at sporting events, or volunteering. While there, allow yourself to fully appreciate the experience.

3. Build Elevation

   Re-watch a movie or TV show that you found especially inspiring because of the goodness of one or more of the characters. Allow yourself to feel the emotion of elevation as you observe people doing positive, strength-based actions for others. Afterward, try to spread your own kindness and compassion.

PRINCIPLE 84

Focus on beauty.

RISK SOMETHING

If you take risks and put yourself on the line, you could create a whole new set of opportunities for the future. You might achieve what you originally set out to do, but you also may unlock doors that you hadn't even considered. You don't need to be ready to take a risk; you can just go for it.

Even if you fall flat on your face, taking a risk will be beneficial. You gain valuable insight and experience from failure. If you do nothing, then nothing will happen. Of course, that's a comfortable approach, but it will limit how much you grow.

Some people hesitate to go after what they want because it leaves them vulnerable and exposed to hurt, disappointment, and even ridicule. You may fear that if you fail, this means you are a failure, but in fact, by taking risks, you will learn to overcome your fears.

PRINCIPLE 85

Take risks.

PRINCIPLE 86

Make your move before you are ready.

PRINCIPLE 87

Failure doesn't equal being defeated.

LEARN SOMETHING NEW

Exploring brings happiness because you are learning something new about the world. Learning is an indispensable tool that nourishes our minds and soothes our soul. It is a necessity for both personal and professional careers as it makes us capable of understanding and handling things in a better way in life.

Learning is a deliberate attempt by the learners to find viable opportunities in their professional world or personal life. The importance of learning is that it helps in building self-confidence as well. When an individual has the desire to learn, they make progress, and this leads to further connections and experiences.

Accept learning as your guiding force if you are interested in developing your growth curve and making the joyful leap. It is a core need that facilitates progress and development through your desire to learn something new.

PRINCIPLE 88

Get a new set of skills.

LISTEN TO MUSIC

I don't sing because I'm happy; I'm happy because I sing."
– William James

Listening to music is a fabulous way to get a hit of dopamine: In a 2011 study published in Nature Neuroscience, McGill University researchers reported that listening to music you love (especially if it gives you "chills") creates a boost in feel-good dopamine.

Listening to music, you enjoy a decrease in levels of the stress hormone cortisol in your body, which counteracts the effects of chronic stress. This is an important finding since stress causes 60% of all our illnesses and disease. One study showed that if people actively participated in making music by playing various percussion instruments and singing, their immune system was boosted even more than if they passively listened. Just start singing!

Create a playlist! Sing!

PRINCIPLE 89

Connect with music.

PRINCIPLE 90

Create your Happy Playlist or sing.

SMILE

Laugh more, look younger. Laugh with a friend

Who hasn't heard the old saying, "Laughter is the best medicine"? Of course, laughter won't treat ongoing health issues. But it CAN help relieve feelings of anxiety or stress and improve a low mood by boosting dopamine and endorphin levels.

According to a small 2017 study Trusted Source looking at 12 young men, social laughter triggered endorphin release. Research from 2011 Trusted Source supports this finding.

So, share that funny video, dust off your joke book, or watch a comedy special with a friend or partner.

Bonding over something hilarious with a loved one might even trigger oxytocin release. Thoughts and feelings were the result of different chemical reactions and changes in the brain.

PRINCIPLE 91

Smile.

TRAVEL AND EXPLORE THE WORLD

Travel is good for lots of things, but it can also increase mental well-being and not just in the short-term. Whether you're traveling for business, on a one-week family holiday, or have sold everything to pursue a life on the road, traveling can make you a happier person by building self-confidence, providing new experiences and memories, breaking routine, and allowing you to meet people from all over the world.

There comes a time when everyone must deal with an unexpected situation when they're on the road. Even if you plan your trip to the letter, things can take a surprise turn. Whatever happens, there is a way around the problem, and knowing that you can deal with these situations is a big boost to self-confidence and, therefore, your happiness.

Most of my top ten joyful experiences have come to my life as I have been traveling or exploring the world. Try it! Travel and explore new territories and places on earth.

PRINCIPLE 92

Explore the world.

CREATE VISION BOARDS

Envision what you want for your life! Visualization is one of the most powerful tools that are available in everyone's arsenal to achieve great success in life. And the use of a vision board has been scientifically proven to be able to increase the activity of visualization through our minds. When we look at the pictures of the things that we want, we will imagine the achievements, the enjoyment, and the fulfillment we get from them.

If you want to become highly successful and to live your dream life, you must be absolutely clear about what you want to achieve.

Success starts with intention. No matter what you want to accomplish in your life, you will first have the intention to achieve it.

When you see yourself accomplishing your goals and living the life you have always desired, you will feel good and motivated. Success and achieving extraordinary results in life is not easy. You need the motivation to take action daily. You need to stay on your course when things are tough. And one way to do this is through the use of vision boards and visualization.

PRINCIPLE 93

Visualize your outcome.

STOP SELF-SABOTAGING YOUR SUCCESS

Your subconscious probably sees self-sabotage as self-preservation, a way to safeguard and defend yourself, even if it's no longer needed. Some of our self-sabotage is so subtle it's easy to miss. We often fail to recognize how our actions are hurting ourselves.

We don't see how our disorganization distracts us, or how we're constantly overthinking all of our decisions, leaving us practically paralyzed with inaction. We don't realize that our reactions to situations end up causing bigger problems in the long run.

Recognize self-sabotaging habits.

The first step to breaking the cycle of self-sabotage is becoming aware of these behaviors. Try looking at your behaviors as an outsider. What self-destructive habits, patterns, and mindsets are holding you back?

Here are a few common self-sabotage habits to be aware of:

- Procrastination: Instead of tackling an important project in a timely manner, you allow yourself to dawdle to the last minute. It's hard to shine when you don't give yourself time to fix mistakes or do a thorough job. Start setting deadlines and mini-deadlines to work toward your objective.
- Negative self-talk/negative thinking: Your inner dialogue is constantly critical, and you always expect the worst outcome. Be kind to yourself! Only expect the best for you!
- Perfectionism: You tell yourself you can't take action until the right time, or believe you need to perfect your skills before you move forward. These are forms of self-sabotage. Perfection is an impossible standard that keeps you from moving forward.
- Self-Doubts: Overthinking leads to the inability to make firm decisions, and that fear prevents actions from taking place. When you make any decision, for better or for worse, you affect change. And it's scary to be responsible for the change. But decisions can have a strong, positive impact, and it's important to remember that. We need to break the assumption that a decision will end up hurting someone's feelings, rocking the boat, or causing friction.

Acknowledge that self-doubt exists, and make an action plan to silence it moving forward. Responding to that negative voice with a healthier inner dialogue will help you develop the mental strength you need to perform at your peak this year and beyond.

PRINCIPLE 94

Avoid self-sabotage.

PRINCIPLE 95

Only doubt your limits.

PRINCIPLE 96

You can do anything your heart wants.

BE MINIMALISTIC

Practicing minimalism is one of the best skills you can have in life in order to be happy. When you learn to be happy with less, you will realize that you can be happy with anything. You will realize that you don't need an expensive car or a luxurious vacation to be happy. You can do more with less.

You can have less and deliver more, have less, and be happier.

In an age of visual, information, and distraction overflow, our minds and eyes crave simplicity, but we are so conditioned to want more and more that we get lost in-between. Simple color palettes, less clutter, more white space, intentional words, less things are not a sign of weakness but can become your strength. When combined, these concepts create a sense of flow and togetherness to help you experience levels of happiness and joy you have never imagined, and they are right in front of you.

PRINCIPLE 97

Less is more.

HOW CAN I MAINTAIN HAPPINESS IN TODAY'S CHALLENGING WORLD?

How can one sustain hope in humanity in the face of human violence and suffering? We were all born on this earth. We might have different DNA, but we are all on this planet together.

Happiness and joy can aid in overcoming life's inevitable adversities and suffering. It doesn't mean that you will not be empathic and perhaps feel sadness. When sadness comes it is important that you distance yourself from that emotion by practicing mindfulness. And then you wear the "happy glasses". This doesn't mean that you will be happy for the death of someone else, for example, but it will mean that you will be able to find the good and the joy out of that sad experience. That you were able to distance yourself from sadness and let it pass through and leave your body-mind-spirit.

How can we remain happy in a world that is constantly bombarding us in our phones and everywhere with information meant to make us feel fear and anger?

So how can we do a better job at stopping our circumstances from hindering our happiness?

Being distressed, and being bothered by small things instantly, is terrible for discipline. You have a goal, you're working, and then thoughts and distress about something external happen.

Reinforce to yourself what is within your control and what is out of your control; if you embrace what is out of your control and accept it, you will experience tranquillity. What is in your control is how you want to feel. Always focus on how you want to feel! Intuitively you will know what to do to get to feel that way. Listen to your heart!

DON'T WORRY BE HAPPY

Refer to the following wording next time you're distressed and distracted:

1. Do you have a problem in your life?
2. No? ► Then don't worry.
3. Yes? ► Can you do something about it?
4. Yes? ► Then don't worry.
5. No? ► Then don't worry.

TAKE THE PATH OF LEAST RESISTANCE

The path of least resistance is also known as "going with the flow". Many think that the path of least resistance means taking no action, staying with crossed arms without doing anything. The path of least resistance is more like being water in a stream; it will always get its way with the least resistance. The stream of water will always find its way.

The path of least resistance does not mean you settle for less. It means taking perfect action. Nature is a true example of the path of least resistance: water, electricity, and wind.

For everything that you want, there is a path of least resistance to help you to it.

You know when you are in the path of least resistance when:

- You get a great idea when you feel good, relaxed, in the parasympathetic nervous system, and very open to receiving.
- You get a glimpse and a feeling of what is coming.

- When you have no doubt, you're in the right place at the right time.
- When you are in harmony, even with the challenges you are facing.

How to know when you are not in the path of least resistance:

- You keep doing the same thing expecting different results.
- You are attached to "how" something will happen instead of the "what" you want to happen.
- When the perspective of your business or a project that you're working on is how much you hate it.
- When you are constantly bothered by something or someone.

Storytime:

One time, in a small Tuscany coast town, there was a lonely old retired man who lived a beautiful small apartment in the rooftop of a building. He would wake up, open his eyes, and get out of bed to feel angry and bothered by the pigeons that would come to his tiled roof to build a nest. Every morning he would plan a new way of keeping the birds away. He would install traps that wouldn't work, allowing the pigeons to build their nest on top of the traps. He would then install metal pigeon spikes, but the birds would just continue to build nests around it and on top of it. His anger would get him operating from his sympathetic nervous system.

He would get so angry every day, chasing them away and even trying to poison them, but it would never work out.

From the building across the street, a beautiful old lady would observe him every day fighting with the pigeons. She was also lonely. She would observe him releasing his anger against the birds; he was so busy with his anger against the pigeons that it was impossible for him to notice her.

The minute he would go to town to run some errands, the birds would come back and build their nest on top of all the junk that he would install to keep them away. His whole tiled roof was filled with traps, junk, and pigeons.

One day when he opened his eyes, clearly tired and tired of the same fight every day, something changed. He went to the hardwood and bought more materials. He looked determined about something.

He arrived at his rooftop apartment and started building something. He was taking his time to build it right until his masterpiece was completed. He built a multilevel wooden structure for the pigeons to build nests in. He removed all the traps, the poison, the spikes, and embraced the pigeons in his life in a new way. The pigeons also loved their new home to the point that they stop nesting on his roof as they now had their own place.

Admiring his creation and how happy the pigeons looked, he felt for the first time in a long time a joyful satisfaction. Looking at the birds, his eyeline found the beautiful old lady who waved at him from the distance. He was shocked by her elegance and beauty. She lifted her teacup and invited him over for tea.

Only when he took the path of least resistance and let go of all his expectations, was he able to shift his emotions and outcome of life. When he released the idea of stopping the birds from coming and instead worked around, he was able to invite new opportunities into his life. His problem was over because he chose to work around it and not let it affect him anymore.

The path of least resistance will help you when facing challenges; it will help you to protect your happiness and joy.

For all that we are, for everything that we are yet to experience, let's all choose the path of least resistance when facing a crisis, let's wear our "happy glasses" and filter our reality with happiness while we continue to make joyful leaps.

PRINCIPLE 98

Take the path of least resistance.

PRINCIPLE 99

Don't worry, be happy.

PRINCIPLE 100

Always focus on how you want to feel.

PART VIII

22 DAYS QUANTUM
JOYFULNESS PROGRAM

QUANTUM JOYFULNESS TRANSFORMATION PLAN

I F YOU MADE it until here, you are probably ready to make the leap by committing to real drastic changes. You are ready to take your life to higher grounds, experiencing superior levels of joy and happiness. We already went through some of the principals that we can apply to our values in order to live a happy life. Now, in order to complete the joyful transformation in a mind-body-spirit way, it is important that everything we are is integrated and working together. Therefore, we will work our body with Quantum Workouts and Quantum Diets.

This 22 days program you are about to embark on will create changes in a cellular, atomic, and DNA way. Making joyful leaps inside your body by cleaning and resetting your DNA, stem cell regeneration, and body shape.

Much information of our traumas is trapped, not only in our DNA but in our body inside fat cells and in the form of toxins. These toxins that might have been ingested throughout our lives are still in our body, sometimes for many years. A detoxifying and cell regenerative diet will enhance the joyful leap by getting rid of what doesn't serve you in your body while enhancing your immune system.

When we are eliminating fat cells and toxins, we will also be releasing the energy, the emotions, and the impact of those toxins in your body. This diet will also elevate and enhance the regeneration of positive practices in your life, because it will also be happening inside your body, within the energy of your atoms.

There is scientific evidence that it takes 21 days to create a new habit or change/transform old habits. For the purpose of this transformation plan, we are going with 22 days because it is a master number.

For the 22 Days Quantum Joyfulness Transformation Program, there are three important elements that we will adopt during these days:

1. **QUANTUM DIETS** - DNA RENEWAL: Immune System & Cellular Regenerator Diet – We are what we eat, and in order to really create impactful change in our lives, we have to also transform drastically what we will intake. There are three diets I suggest for you to try, "The Quantum Initiation Diet", "The Quantum Sailor Diet", and "The Quantum Body Reset Diet". Make sure you go with the diet that resonates with you from the options I suggest to you. It is important you listen to your body and adapt the diet to your special needs; remember to consult your nutritionist before starting any dietary program. But these ones, I suggest, are specifically designed to stimulate cell regeneration and DNA rewiring because they include fasting methods.

2. **QUANTUM WORKOUTS: Exercises + Mantras** - Yes, you have heard right, let's move the energy of our body and become our own portal. We will combine mantras with a workout routine. The exercises and routines go from basic to more advanced. You can also create your own routine as long as you incorporate mantras to each of the exercises.

3. **JOURNALING: Exercising Happy and joyful principles** Every day during the 22 days, whenever you feel like activating your emotional radar, check in with your emotions and the ones of those around you. Write them down. At the end of the day, write about your day. You will keep track of everything that you are experiencing and events that stimulate you to generate new questions. Detail in writing one positive experience you experienced each day. You will start finding reasons to be joyfully happy every day more and more! This will help you find meaning in the activities of the day, rather than just noticing the task itself.

Also, it is important that each day you write one reason for you to be grateful each day. You will also write about **RANDOM ACTS OF KINDNESS** you have done during the day. As small as it might seem every day, you can practice a random act of kindness, even if it is just holding the door for the person behind you. Watering plants, calling an old friend, reaching out.

You can document the changes you are starting to see in your body as you progress in the body, and the changes you are experiencing in your life as you are making the joyful leap. Writing about all this new way of being joyful and feeling the bliss of life every day. After the 22 days, keep writing, don't let it die.

QUANTUM DIETS

* **R**EMEMBER TO CONSULT A MEDICAL PROFESSIONAL before starting any kind of diet program, including this one, especially if you have a pre-existing condition consult your main doctor.

The following diets are all meant to take you to a place of physical and cellular regeneration. There are different levels and intensities; you can select the diet that works most for you. And remember, this is just a suggestion to inspire you to start in your path, but ideally, you will get to the point of knowing yourself and your body that you will be able to create diets that work especially for you and your blood type. Get a test! Know your blood type and find out the best nutrients for you!

QUANTUM INITIATION DIET

DAY 1 - 5	JUICE FAST
DAY 6 - 22	VEGAN DIET

THE QUANTUM SAILOR DIET

DAY 1 - 2	WATER FAST
DAY 3 - 6	JUICE FAST
DAY 7 – 9	RAW VEGAN DIET
DAY 10 - 22	VEGAN DIET

THE QUANTUM BODY RESET DIET

DAY 1	WATER FAST
DAY 2 -4	SOFT DRY FAST
DAY 5 - 10	JUICE FAST
DAY 11 - 16	RAW VEGAN DIET
DAY 17 - 22	VEGAN DIET

Our ancestors didn't have a fridge and food at their fingertips. It was natural for them to have cycles of feast and famine, and going without food for a few days was not uncommon at times. There were also seasonal changes with ample food in late summer and autumn and less to eat in winter.

Our bodies are designed to burn either carbohydrates (i.e., sugars) or fat for energy. The master-switch that flips the fuel source from carbs to fat is insulin. When insulin is high, which it is in the presence of excess blood sugar, the little powerhouses in our cells - the mitochondria - will burn sugar. Only when insulin is low enough will mitochondria switch to burning fat.

Doesn't our body prefer burning sugar? No, it's a choice made out of necessity. Because high blood sugar is toxic to our body, it is the cell's first priority to get all the abundant sugar out of the bloodstream into the cells. In the cell, all the sugar needed for energy is handed down to the mitochondria, where it is burned. Excess sugar, which is not needed, is converted to fat and stored in fat cells for later use.

This is one of the two main reasons why people experience flu-like symptoms or headaches the first few days on a fast or when switching to a low carb ketogenic diet. The body has to re-learn the ability to produce all the enzymes needed to burn fat as energy.

But only through a fasting period our body cells regenerates massively, we eliminate a vast amount of toxins by eliminating fat cells. Our immune system is boosted, and our energy is renewed.

That is why it is a good idea to support the excretion of these toxins through the urine and stool during a fast. The first is supported by ample intake of water, the latter by supporting the peristaltic motion in the intestine. The addition of electrolytes or salt to the drinking water can further help.

SOFT DRY FASTING

Soft dry fast is where you brush your teeth, take a shower, and wash your face. On the other hand, a hard, dry fast is a fast where you do not come in touch with water at all. In the state where your body doesn't get food or water, it starts the process of utilizing everything available for energy, not only for food but also water - that too at the cellular level. This sort of extreme fasting will obviously put your body in distress. And it gets more stressed out to find more water. This eventually makes your body work harder to utilize cells that are not useful and are inefficient. It also leads to autophagy, which is your body's natural process of recycling old and damaged cells to get energy. It creates new, improved cells and eliminates the bad ones. As a result, only the strong cells survive a natural progression.

WATER FASTING

Water Fast, also called Wet Fast, is a type of fasting in which the practitioner consumes water only and no food whatsoever. During a water fast, you are not allowed to eat or drink anything besides water.

Most people drink two to three liters of water per day during a water fast. When we enter the state of fasting, the remaining carbs will be used up. The body will then switch to burning fat. At the same time, the metabolic rate goes up, not down, as happens in a state of caloric restriction (diets with low-calorie intake). This leads to weight loss.

In fact, up to 50% of our energy is required to digest food. In a fast, this energy is freed up from the digestive process and can now be used to heal and regenerate. The body knows best where healing is needed most.

After 24-36 hours, sick and weakened cells will be driven into cell death, taken apart, and recycled into new cells through processes called apoptosis and autophagy. An average human adult loses 50 to 70 billion cells each day through apoptosis. This rate is strongly increased by fasting.

The next step in the fasting process is a sharp increase in stem cell production and activation. The number of new stem cells and the level of HGH, the human growth hormone, significantly surge during days 3-5 of a fast and then afterward decline again. Newer research has shown that a huge amount of new white blood cells are produced during that time of increased stem cell generation, thereby strengthening the immune system.

Besides burning fat, weight loss, and an increased immune system due to the reproduction of stem cells, fasting has a lot of additional health benefits, from reducing inflammation, rebalancing the gut microbiome and hormones, protecting the brain from adverse changes associated with Alzheimer's, Parkinson's and other neurological diseases, reducing the risk of cancer and decreasing the rate of aging and up-regulating the processes of cell maintenance and repair.

HOW TO DEAL WITH HUNGER DURING THE FAST

Hunger comes and goes in waves around your normal mealtimes. It is best to drink water when a hunger feeling comes up. Add a pinch of sea salt to the water for electrolytes. Drinking water will stretch your stomach and thus decrease ghrelin, the hunger hormone. Contrary to belief, the hunger feeling will not continuously rise. Two hours after your normal mealtime, the ghrelin level, and with it, the hunger feeling will be the same, no matter whether you had something to eat or are fasting. The longer you fast, the more the feeling of hunger will decrease.

*When breaking the fast, for the first two days, eat low fiber fruits and vegetables. Some low fibers fruits and vegetables include cucumber, avocado, tomatoes, strawberries, blueberries, lettuce, etc.

JUICE FAST

Juice fasting, also known as juice cleansing, is a diet in which a person consumes only fruit and vegetable juices while abstaining from solid food consumption. It is used for detoxification, an alternative medicine treatment, and is often part of detox diets.

Raw juices are extremely rich in alkaline elements, and this is highly beneficial in normalizing acid-alkaline balance in the blood and tissues. The juices extracted from raw fruits and vegetables require no digestion, and almost all their vital nutrients are assimilated directly in the bloodstream.

Studies have shown that fasting induces cellular repair, such as removing waste material from cells. There are beneficial changes in several genes related to the protection of disease and longevity. Fasting induces hormonal changes which facilitates weight loss.

In a 2014 study on intermittent fasting, it was shown that people lost about 3-8% of their weight over 24 weeks. In the same study, it was shown that people lost a lot of belly fat, too. The harmful kind of fat in the abdominal cavity, which leads to disease and reduces insulin resistance. This lowers blood sugar levels and protects you against type 2 diabetes. Studies have also shown that fasting reduces oxidative stress and inflammation. Fasting and caloric restriction, in general, reduces blood pressure, cholesterol levels, and inflammatory markers.

When we fast, the body breaks down dysfunctional proteins inside the cells, which makes us both feel and look better: we literally change and cleanse from deep within the cells. Fasting improves various metabolic functions that are good for brain health. In one study on rats that fasted every other day, they lived 83% longer than those rats who did not.

*When breaking the fast, for the first two days, eat low fiver fruits and vegetables. Some low fivers fruits and vegetables include, cucumber, avocado, tomatoes, strawberries, blueberries, lettuce, etc.

RAW VEGAN DIET

A raw food vegan diet consists of unprocessed raw vegan foods that have not been heated above 115 F (46 C). Food cooked above this temperature have lost their enzymes and thus a significant amount of their nutritional value and are harmful to the body, whereas uncooked foods provide living enzymes and proper nutrition.

Some of the benefits of eating raw foods, include weight loss, more energy, clear skin, improved digestion, and improved overall health. Raw foodists also drink fresh fruit and vegetable juices and include herbal teas in their diet as well. Most people who follow a raw vegan diet include a limited amount of foods that have undergone some processing, as long as the processing involved does not involve heating the food over 115 degrees. The raw vegan diet excludes all animal products, including meat, eggs, and dairy.

Coming the period of cellular regeneration with water fast and juice fast, the raw vegan diet gives you the support to train your body's new cells to breakdown food that is good for them.

VEGAN DIET

Veganism is defined as a way of living that attempts to exclude all forms of animal exploitation and cruelty, whether for food, clothing, or any other purpose. The difference between raw vegan is that with a vegan diet, you can heat and cook meals without restrictions. Some of the benefits of a vegan diet, include weight loss, low cancer risk, low diabetes risk, becoming more sustainable, and many more. The vegan diet excludes all animal products, including meat, eggs, and dairy.

With this diet, you will be reaffirming your happiness, and the joy you will be activating in your life on a quantum level inside your body. Your body will feel and be that change also.

Plant-based diets like these will rewire your body's functionality while freeing you from animal cruelty consumption and hyper-processed foods. Not only will you be contributing to the wellbeing of the environment, but you will be saving animal lives and practicing values like kindness and compassion just in your diet.

Focus on whole foods that are vegan and try to limit your junk vegan food intake. At the end of the day, it's still junk food.

You will be making the joyful leap aligned with a diet that supports and enhances your change at a quantum level.

Again, this is not written in stone; you must do what is better for your body. This is just a diet I am suggesting to you in order to go to a process of regeneration at a quantum level incorporating your mind-body-spirit.

QUANTUM WORKOUTS

Choose one of these 3 Quantum workouts to adopt during the 22 days transformation plan. Remember that you can also create your own; always be honest with what your body wants. These are just simply the ones I am suggesting for you to take, but ideally, you will get to the point of awareness with your body that you will create your own workouts. Remember to always listen to your body and know what is best for you. Pick one of the LEVELS that resonate for you:

1. BASIC LEVEL (11 Minutes) - Consists of a workout set with ELEVEN activities matched with 11 mantras. This option is perfect for someone getting back into a fitness experience.
2. INTERMEDIATE (22 Minutes) - Consists in a workout set with TWENTY-TWO activities matched with 22 mantras. This option is perfect for someone with some fitness experience or just looking to adopt a physical discipline that brings results.
3. ADVANCED - (33 Minutes) - Consists of a workout set with THIRTY-THREE activities matched with 33 mantras. This option is ideal for someone with fitness goals and bringing notable athletic results.

*DON'T FORGET TO CONSULT A MEDICAL PROFESSIONAL before starting any kind of fitness program, including this one.

The key is to practice your physical discipline first thing in the morning. Why? Because it will give you a sense of accomplishment in the early hours of your day, it will also help you set the intention and reprogram your thoughts for your day. None of these physical disciplines require you to buy anything as they are designed for you to do then anywhere without a gym membership. You could get a yoga mat if you prefer to, but it is not necessary.

All of these three quantum workout sets are a combination of CrossFit, Yoga, and Tai-Chi. Don't worry if you don't have experience in any of them as all of them are easy to learn and memorize. Is important you stretch your body before starting your workout and incorporate after the workout a 10 to 30 minutes of cardiovascular exercises. You can do cardio by running, jugging, swimming, using the jumping rope among other exercises. Cardiovascular exercises will help you to releasetoxins, and dead cells.

The goal of the diet, mantras, and workouts combination is to make a joyful quantum leap towards happiness by combining Mind-Body-Spirit in an energetic and physical practice.

The idea is that through each exercise during the routine, you will be repeating the assigned mantra for each exercise.

RISE AND SHINE

Practicing the physical routine is important as it will right away grant you the feeling of accomplishment in the early hours of the day and work on your self-discipline. Setting-up the day for success. **Set an intention for the day at the end of the quantum Workout.**

Try doing one minute per exercise; if you feel like you want to do more time in some of them, feel free to do so. What's important is that you connect with your body and listen to what it really wants.

CREATE YOUR QUANTUM WORKOUT SPACE

Your workout space is your "sacred space", the "altar" of your body-mind-spirit. Make sure there is enough space to move, to dance, to stretch, and to exercise. It is important that you have at least one mirror, if not several, that allow you to see your own reflection as you work out and do your routines.

EMBARKING THE QUANTUM BODY ROUTINE (11 MINUTES)

1. **SUN SALUTATION** "I AM GRATEFUL FOR THE BLISS OF OPENING MY EYES TODAY."
2. **CRANE TAKES FLIGHT** "MY HAPPINESS ELEVATES EVERY DAY MORE."
3. **KAMPALA BIATATI BREATHING (CROSSED LEGS)** "MY VOICE IS OPENLY RESONATING IN THE UNIVERSE."
4. **ALTERNATE NOSTRIL BREATHING** "MY BODY IS ALWAYS HAPPY TO REGENERATE MY ATOMS, MY CELLS, AND DNA."
5. **CAT-COW POSE** "MY JOY GIVES ME THE WISDOM TO THRIVE."
6. **HERO POSE + SHOULDER ROTATION** "WE ARE OUR OWN HEROES; THEREFORE, MY HEART IS OPEN."
7. **WARRIOR POSE** "OM"
8. **TRIANGLE POSE** "THE WISDOM AND HEALING OF MY BODY IN ANCIENT."
9. **WESTERN POSE** "I AM ENOUGH, INDEPENDENT, AND COMPLETE BECAUSE I LOVE MYSELF."
10. **ONE-LEGGED SEATED TWIST** "TODAY, I WILL MAKE JOYFUL LEAPS."
11. **DANCE** "I AM FREE."

QUANTUM SAILOR ROUTINE (22 MINUTES)

1. **SUN SALUTATION** "I AM GRATEFUL FOR THE BLISS OF OPENING MY EYES TODAY."
2. **CRANE TAKES FLIGHT** "MY HAPPINESS ELEVATES EVERY DAY MORE."
3. **KAMPALA BIATATI BREATHING (CROSSED LEGS)** "MY VOICE IS OPENLY RESONATING IN THE UNIVERSE."
4. **ALTERNATIVE NOSTRIL BREATHING** "MY BODY IS ALWAYS HAPPY TO REGENERATE MY ATOMS, MY CELLS, AND DNA."
5. **CAT-COW POSE** "MY JOY GIVES ME THE WISDOM TO THRIVE."
6. **HERO POSE + SHOULDER ROTATION** "WE ARE OUR OWN HEROES; THEREFORE, MY HEART IS OPEN."
7. **WARRIOR POSE** "OM"

8. **TRIANGLE POSE** "THE WISDOM AND HEALING OF MY BODY IS ANCIENT."
9. **PLANK** "I AM WILLING TO TAKE RISKS."
10. **30 PUSHUPS** "I HAVE STAMINA."
11. **CHILD POSE** "I AM ALWAYS FUN AND PLAYFUL LIKE AN ETERNAL CHILD."
12. **30 ABS** "I GET STRONGER EVERY DAY."
13. **WESTERN POSITION** "I AM ENOUGH, INDEPENDENT, AND COMPLETE BECAUSE I LOVE MYSELF."
14. **ONE-LEGGED SEATED** "TODAY, I WILL CREATE MANY JOYFUL MEMORIES."
15. **BRIDGE POSE** "I AM WHAT I HAVE ALWAYS DREAMT OF."
16. **BOW POSE** "I HAVE A VISION AND PURPOSE IN MY LIFE."
17. **FORWARD FOLD (FOLDING UP)** "I AM GRATEFUL."
18. **SNAKE CREEPS DOWN** "I AM FERTILE."
19. **THE GOLDEN ROOSTER** "I THRIVE IN THE WORLD."
20. **30 SQUATS** "I GOT THIS."
21. **DANCE** "I AM FREE."
22. **TREE POSE** "I AM IN BALANCE, READY TO START MY DAY."

THE QUANTUM ROYAL ROUTINE (33 MINUTES)

1. **SUN SALUTATION** "I AM GRATEFUL FOR THE BLISS OF OPENING MY EYES TODAY."
2. **CRANE TAKES FLIGHT** "MY HAPPINESS ELEVATES EVERY DAY MORE."
3. **CLOUD HANDS** "I AM IN SYNCHRONICITY WITH LIFE."
4. **GRASPING THE BIRDS TAIL** "I AM AN EXTENSION OF THE POWER OF THE UNIVERSE."
5. **NECK ROTATIONS** "I AM FLEXIBLE."
6. **KAMPALA BIATATI BREATHING (CROSSED LEGS)** "MY VOICE IS OPENLY RESONATING IN THE UNIVERSE."
7. **ALTERNATIVE NOSTRIL BREATHING** "MY BODY IS ALWAYS HAPPY TO REGENERATE MY ATOMS, MY CELLS, AND DNA."
8. **HERO POSE + SHOULDER ROTATION** "WE ARE OUR OWN HEROES; THEREFORE, MY HEART IS OPEN."
9. **CAT-COW POSE** "MY JOY GIVES ME THE WISDOM TO THRIVE."
10. **WARRIOR POSE** "OM"

11. **TRIANGLE POSE** "THE WISDOM AND HEALING OF MY BODY IS ANCIENT."
12. **KING PIGEON POSE** "I AM A CONFIDENT LEADER."
13. **BOAT POSE** "I CAN DO ANYTHING I PUT MY MIND INTO."
14. **PLANK** "I AM WILLING TO TAKE RISKS."
15. **100 PUSHUPS** "I HAVE STAMINA."
16. **CHILD POSE** "I AM ALWAYS FUN AND PLAYFUL LIKE AN ETERNAL CHILD."
17. **100 ABS** "I GET STRONGER EVERY DAY."
18. **WESTERN POSITION** "I AM ENOUGH, INDEPENDENT, AND COMPLETE BECAUSE I LOVE MYSELF."
19. **SHOULDER STAND** "I ASK, I BELIEVE, I RECEIVE."
20. **PLOW POSE** "I CREATE ABUNDANT OPPORTUNITIES."
21. **ONE-LEGGED SEATED** "TODAY, I WILL CREATE MANY JOYFUL MEMORIES."
22. **BRIDGE POSE** "I AM WHAT I HAVE ALWAYS DREAMT OF."
23. **BOW POSE** "I HAVE A VISION AND PURPOSE IN MY LIFE."
24. **FORWARD FOLD (FOLDING UP)** "I AM GRATEFUL."
25. **SNAKE CREEPS DOWN** "I AM FERTILE."
26. **THE GOLDEN ROOSTER** "I THRIVE IN THE WORLD."
27. **HIGH HEELS KICK** "MY HAPPINESS IS UNCONDITIONAL."
28. **RISE AND SINK** "HAPPINESS GROUNDS ME."
29. **100 SQUATS** "I GOT THIS."
30. **LUNGE TWIST** "I ASCEND TOWARDS JOY EVERY DAY."
31. **CHAIR POSE** "I AM SITTING IN THE THRONE OF LIGHT."
32. **DANCE** "I AM FREE."
33. **TREE POSE** "I AM BALANCED AND READY TO START MY DAY."

YOU CAN ALSO CREATE YOUR OWN ROUTINE

In order to create your own routine, just write down a list of exercises from any physical activity you would like to apply to your routine. Write next to each exercise the "mantra" or "intention" of each of them. Repeat the mantra, respectively, for each exercise. Set a time limit for each exercise. Practice your routine every morning when you wake up.

THE EXERCISES

SUN SALUTATION

MANTRA: "I am grateful for the bliss of opening my eyes today."
REPEAT FOR 3 MINUTES

Remember to breathe during this and all exercises: breathe out as you move towards Mother Earth, breathe in as you raise yourself to stand tall.

a) Stand in a Mountain Pose with your palms together in Prayer Position, thumbs touching your heart.

b) Inhale and reach your arms up and slightly back. Gaze toward the sky, feeling a long stretch from neck to feet.

c) Exhale and fold forward from your hips. Touch your hands to the floor. Bend your knees slightly if you feel inflexible.

d) With your hands on the floor, inhale and extend your right leg back in a lunge. You can put your knee down or keep it lifted.

e) Bring your left back and exhale, lowering your knees and claves to the floor.

f) With an inhale, press your palms into the floor and straighten your gaze up. This is the Cobra Pose.

g) Exhale and lift your bottom to the sky. Straighten your leg. You will be in an inverted "V" position. This is Downward-Facing Dog Pose.

h) Inhale and bring your right foot forward, back into a lunge.

i) Exhale and bring your left foot to meet your right in a Forward Fold.

j) Inhale and roll your upper body up to standing.

k) Exhale in a Mountain Pose, hands to Prayer Position.

l) *For 10 sun salutations, do 5 with the right leg first, then 5 with the left.*

CRANE TAKES FLIGHT

MANTRA: "My happiness elevates every day more."
REPEAT FOR ONE MINUTE

a) Start in Horse Stand with your feet parallel, shoulder-width apart, and bend your knees.
b) Inhale. Stretching your knees, feeling as if your heart is opening when your arms raise up sideways, like a bird ready to fly.

c) When exhaling, push the palm of your hands sideways, pushing conflicts and negativity away as you bend your knees. Repeat again.

COULD HANDS

MANTRA: "I am in synchronicity with life."
REPEAT FOR ONE MINUTE

a) Stand in Horse Stand, feet shoulder-width apart, feet parallel and facing 12:00. Imagine head lifted from the crown, chin tucked in slightly, eyes forward and relaxed, shoulders relaxed. Right palm facing body in line with the center chest at shoulder height. Left elbow below level with the left hand's palm facing down with fingers pointing to 3:00 and slightly curved.
b) Inhale. Rotate your torso to the right and transfer your weight to the right leg, keeping your knees slightly bent.
c) Exhale. Extend the right arm as if drawing a curve until the right-hand palm facing down at the shoulder level. Your left arm palm elevates facing up until aligned with the right elbow. At the same time, the left leg moves right next to the right one and grounds into the floor. The right elbow below level with the right hand's palm facing down, fingers point to 9:00 and slightly

curved. The left hand's palm is at the right shoulder level facing inwards.

d) Inhale. Torso rotates left, and you transfer your weight to the left leg, keeping your knees bent.

e) Exhale. Extend the left arm as if drawing a curve until the left-hand palm is facing down at the shoulder level. Your right arm palm elevates facing up until aligned with the left elbow. At the same time, the right leg opens right as if in Horse Stand. The left elbow below level with the left hand's palm facing down, fingers point to 3:00 and slightly curved. The right hand's palm is at the left shoulder lever facing inwards.

If you feel like it, you can repeat on the opposite side.

A   B   C1   C2

C3   D   E1   E2

GRAB THE BIRDS TAIL

MANTRA: "I am an extension of the power of the universe."
REPEAT FOR ONE MINUTE

a) As if coming from Horse Stand, relax the left leg and fully sit into the right leg. Turn waist towards 12:00, forming a ball with hands, right hand on top. The legs stay grounded in the same position without lifting or moving the foot from the ground.

b) Exhaling. Turn your waist slightly left as you gently transfer your weight forward into the left leg. Carry and push the ball of light with the right hand, until your left arm is 90 degrees with the left palm facing up. The left elbow is aligned with your left side chest and the right palm that faces down.

c) Inhaling. Rotate your left palm to the right until it faces down. Then gently move it passed your right shoulder while transferring weight into the right leg. The left palm is following the right palm (facing down) movement. As if you are drawing a "bowl" with the flat bottom part in front of your pelvis. Your left-hand reaches out while the right-hand curves until the outside Carpals of your right hand are touching the inside Carpals of your left hand.

d) Exhaling. Slowly transfer all weight towards the left leg while right-hand pushes in "chopping hand" style the left until both hands are dissolved and released with both arms stretched, aligned with palms facing down.

e) Inhaling. As if creating a circle with them, the hands facing down elevate at the level of your eyebrows. They circle in your face, and the palms push out at your chest level as you exhale.

If you feel like it, you can repeat on the opposite side.

A   B1   B2   B3

NECK ROTATIONS

MANTRA: "I am flexible."
REPEAT FOR ONE MINUTE

a) Stand tall with feet shoulder-width apart. Let arms hang down at sides. Shoulders should be relaxed and drooping down. This is the starting position.
b) Begin the exercise by tilting the head back. Next, slowly roll your neck in a circular motion to the left for 30 seconds.
c) Next, reverse movement and roll neck to the right for 30 seconds.

KAMPALABHATI BREATHING (CROSSED LEGS)

MANTRA: "My voice is openly resonating in the universe."
REPEAT FOR ONE MINUTE

a) In your cross-legged position, rest your hands on your knees.
b) Through your nose only, take a deep breath and exhale quickly, making a "puff out" sound.
c) Focus on a forceful exhale, not on the inhale. Your chest will rise with every exhale.
d) Perform for one minute.

ALTERNATIVE NOSTRIL BREATHING

MANTRA: "My body is always happy to regenerate my atoms, my cells, and DNA."
REPEAT FOR ONE MINUTE

a) For this exercise, you will also breathe through your nose only. With your right thumb, close off your right nostril.
b) Change to close off the left nostril. Inhale through that right nostril.
c) Change to close off the right nostril with your right thumb and exhale through your left nostril. Inhale through that left nostril.
d) Change to close off the left nostril with your right forefinger and exhale through the right nostril. Your inhale should be through the same nostril, exhales through the opposite nostril.
e) Do each side five times before repeating again for one minute.

HERO POSE + SHOULDER ROTATION

MANTRA: "We are our own heroes; therefore, my heart is open."
REPEAT FOR ONE MINUTE

   a) SIt on your knees with your arms relaxed on the side.
   b) Rotate your shoulder backward 10 times.
   c) Rotate your shoulders forward 10 times.
   d) Repeat for one minute.

CAT-COW POSE

MANTRA: "My joy gives me the wisdom to thrive."
REPEAT FOR ONE MINUTE

a) On your hands and knees, gently lift your belly button towards your spine to make your back flat. Your neck should be long and the top of your head forward.
b) Simultaneously, lift your head up and your bottom up, curving your back in a slight "U" shape.
c) Take 5 deep breaths.
d) Round your spine in an upside-down "U" shape.
e) Drop your head and gaze at your navel.
f) Take 5 deep breaths.
g) Repeat for one minute.

WARRIOR POSE

MANTRA: "OM"
REPEAT FOR ONE MINUTE

a) Stand tall in Mountain Pose, then step up with your feet wide apart.
b) With your hands on your hips, turn your right leg and foot out 90 degrees.
c) Square your chest in the direction of your right leg.
d) Inhale and lift your arms above your head. Bring your palms together.
e) Exhale and bend your right knee to a 90-degree angle.
f) Take 5 deep breaths.
g) Straighten your right leg and return to Mountain Pose.
h) Repeat on the other side.
i) Take 5 deep breaths.

TRIANGLE POSE

MANTRA: "The wisdom and healing of my body is ancient."
REPEAT FOR ONE MINUTE

a) From Mountain Pose, step your feet wide apart. Make sure that your hips are facing forward.
b) Turn your right leg, including your thigh, knee, and foot, out 90 degrees.
c) Turn your left leg in about 15 degrees.
d) Raise your arms to shoulder level straight out, with your palms facing down. Inhale and stretch your upper body over your right leg.
e) Exhale as you place your right hand on your right shin. Keep your chest open.
f) Raise your left arm towards the sky, with your palm facing forward. Gaze at your hand.
g) Take 5 deep breaths.
h) Return to standing.
i) Pivot your feet and do the other side.
j) Take 5 deep breaths.

KING PIGEON POSE

MANTRA: "I am a confident leader."
REPEAT FOR ONE MINUTE

a) Start on your hands and knees.
b) Slide your right knee forward toward your left hand and lay it down, so your knee is facing out. Your foot should be underneath your chest.
c) Press your palms into the floor and keep your arms straight. Your chest should be forward, along with your head.
d) Take 5 deep breaths.
e) Move back to your hands and knees.
f) Do the other side.
g) Take 5 deep breaths.

BOAT POSE

MANTRA: "I can do anything I put my mind into"
REPEAT FOR ONE MINUTE

a) Sit with your knees bent.
b) Keep your abs firm and lift your legs.
c) Straighten your legs.

d) Reach your arms past your knees. If you need help balancing, lightly hold your thighs.
e) Take 5 deep breaths.
f) Bend your knees and put your feet back on the floor.
g) Lay back and relax.

PLANK

MANTRA: "I am willing to take risks."
HOLD FOR ONE MINUTE

a) Plant hands directly under your shoulders (slightly wider than shoulder-width).
b) Ground toes into the floor and squeeze your glutes to stabilize your body. Your head should be in line with your back and legs.
c) Hold the position for one minute.

PUSHUPS

MANTRA: "I have stamina."

a) Plant hands directly under your shoulders (slightly wider than shoulder-width).
b) Ground toes into the floor and squeeze your glutes to stabilize your body. Your head should be in line with your back and legs.
c) When flexing arms and going to the ground, exhale. When pushing up and straightening your arms inhale.
d) Repeat 50 times if you are Intermediate, and 100 times if you are advanced.

CHILD POSE

MANTRA: "I always have fun as I am playful like an eternal child."
HOLD FOR ONE MINUTE

a) Sit on your knees and reach your arms out in front of you, folding your torso over your thighs. Keep your bottom down.
b) With flat palms, spread your fingers wide. Your face should be close to the floor.
c) Take 5 deep breaths.

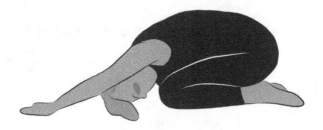

ABS

MANTRA: "I get stronger every day."

a) Lie down on the floor on your back and bend your knees, placing your hands behind your head or across your chest.
b) Pull your belly button towards your spine in preparation for the movement.
c) Slowly contract your abdominals, bringing your shoulder blades about 1 or 2 inches off the floor.
d) Exhale as you come up and keep your neck straight, chin up.
e) Hold at the top of the movement for a few microseconds.
f) Slowly lower back down, but don't relax all the way.
g) Repeat 50 times if you are Intermediate, and 100 times if you are advanced.

WESTERN'S POSE

MANTRA: "I am enough, independent, and complete because I love myself."

HOLD FOR ONE MINUTE

a) Sit with your legs straight out in front of you.
b) Reach out and touch your toes. If you feel inflexible at first, bend your knees slightly.
c) Take 10 deep breaths.

SHOULDER STANDS

MANTRA: "I ask, I believe, I receive."
HOLD FOR ONE MINUTE

a) Lie on your back. Bend your knees and lift your feet off the floor.
b) Support your lower back with your hands.
c) As you lift your legs up toward the ceiling, your bottom will raise as well.
d) Straighten your legs and point your toes to the sky. You will be resting on your shoulder.
e) Take 5 deep breaths.
f) Slowly roll back down until you are lying flat. Release your arms.

PLOW POSE

MANTRA: "I create abundant opportunities."
HOLD FOR ONE MINUTE

a) Lie flat on your back.
b) Move your legs upward until they make a right angle with your upper body.
c) Support your lower back with your hands and lift your bottom up. Your shoulders will remain touching the floor.
d) Bring your legs over your head until your feet touch the floor past your head. Try to keep your legs straight.
e) Bring your arms away from your bac, towards the floor, palms down.
f) Take 5 deep breaths.
g) Roll your body carefully down until you're lying flat.

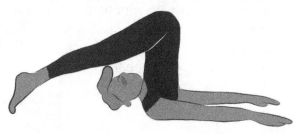

ONE-LEGGED SEATED TWIST

MANTRA: "Today, I will create many joyful memories."
ALTERNATE BOTH SIDES IN ONE MINUTE

    a)   Sit with your legs out in front of you.

    b)   Bend your right knee and place your right foot over your straight left leg.

    c)   Place your elbow on the inside of your bent right leg. Your palm is in a "wave" position. Press your elbow against your knee so you can feel the twist in your waist.

    d)   Take 5 deep breaths.

    e)   Switch sides.

BRIDGE POSE

MANTRA: "I am what I have always dreamt of."
HOLD FOR ONE MINUTE

    a)   Lie on your back with your knees bent, feet on the floor, hips' distance apart.

    b)   Lift up onto your toes.

    c)   Support your lower back with your hands and lift your bottom up. Your shoulders will remain touching the floor.

    d)   Take 5 deep breaths,

    e)   Gently lower your bottom to the floor.

BOW POSE

MANTRA: "I have vision and purpose in my life."
HOLD FOR ONE MINUTE

a) Lie on your stomach.
b) Flex your feet and bend your knees.
c) Lift your feet up and reach back for them with your hands.
d) Holding your ankles, lift your legs. If you can't reach your ankles at first, just reach your arms back and your legs up.
e) Take 5 deep breaths.

FORWARD FOLD (FOLDING UP)

MANTRA: "I am grateful."
HOLD FOR ONE MINUTE

a) Exhale. From Mountain Pose, fold forward.
b) Try to keep your legs straight. If you feel inflexible, bend your knees slightly.
c) Bend your elbows out to the sides, laying one forearm on top of the other.
d) Make fists and squeeze them.
e) Tale 10 deep breaths.
f) Release your hands, arms, head, and let them hang on the floor.
g) Inhale. Roll up vertebrae per vertebrae with a round back and stand in Mountain Pose.

SNAKE CREEPS DOWN

MANTRA: "I am Fertile"
HOLD FOR ONE MINUTE

a) Sit on your bent left leg with toes pointing 9:00. Your right leg relaxed and straight with the toes pointing at 1:00. Your torso, with straightened left-arm and straight palm in 90 degrees facing to 9:00. Your right arm is straight with "hook hands" pointing to your right foot.

b) Exhale. Your left-hand fans roundly inwards until it is facing down straight, pointing at 9:00. At the same time, your right leg completely bends as low as you can, until your left leg is straight. Your right "hook hand" remains the same.

c) Inhale. Your left palm leads the movement upward, while your right "hook hand" follows the movement. Your whole-body weight transfers to your left leg, and your body assumes "The Golden Rooster" stand.

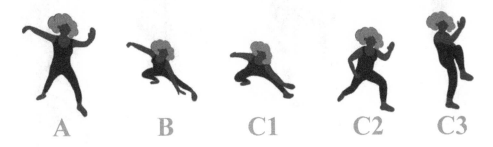

A   B   C1   C2   C3

Reset and repeat.

THE GOLDEN ROOSTER

MANTRA: "I thrive in the world."
REPEAT FOR ONE MINUTE

Golden Rooster, commonly known as "Golden Rooster Stands on One Leg" has a more complete name, which is," the golden rooster stands on one leg to announce the dawn." In the Western Mystery Traditions, the rooster is a metaphor for enlightenment. When the rooster sees the first rays of light in the morning, he stands on one leg to announce to the world the light has come.

a) Start in Horse Stand with both palms facing down at pelvic level and in front of your pelvis's sides.

b) Inhale. With your weight on the left leg, raise your right leg so that your thigh is horizontal & the foot hangs relaxed. At the same time, raise up the right arm with the elbow bent to 90°and relax the Left arm with left palm relaxed facing down, next to your left hip. If possible, bring your knee up to your elbow. Hold the position.

c) Exhale. When ready to come out of the hold, step forward with your right leg, shifting your weight to the right leg.

d) Repeat on the opposite side.

A   B   C   D

HIGH HEELS KICK

MANTRA: "My happiness is unconditional."

a) Inhale. Sitting your weight forward on your left leg, while the right leg is gently behind your right shoulder. With your arms, you create an "X" form shield, with the right arm on top of the left arm. Your left toes and your torso face 9:00.

b) Exhale. As your arms open, your right leg comes from behind and kicks high your right-hand palm, while left-hand palm faces back to your 7:00.

c) After the high kick, finish that exhale with your right leg landing forward into the ground. From your ankles to the toes.

d) Reset and do the other side. Loop and do both sides back-to-back.

| A | B | C | D |

RISE AND SINK

MANTRA: "Happiness grounds me".
HOLD FOR ONE MINUTE

a) Inhale. Start in Horse Stand with arms relaxed and straight, lifting gently until reaching a 90-degree angle with palms relaxed facing down. Your Legs start bent and straighten as you inhale.
b) Exhale. Invert the same movement as you come down and sink down your knees.

| A1 | A2 | A3 | B |

SQUATS

MANTRA: "I got this."

a) Stand facing forward with your chest up.
b) Place your feet shoulder-width apart or slightly wider.
c) Extend your hands straight out in front of you to help keep your balance. You can place your hands in Prayer Position or place them behind your head.
d) Bend your knees and hips, sticking your butt out like if you're sitting into an imaginary chair. Keep your chest lifted and your spine neutral, avoiding letting your spine go round.
e) Squat down as low as you can, keeping your head and chest lifted.
f) Keep your body tight and push through your heels to bring yourself back to the starting position.

Repeat 50 times if you are Intermediate, and 100 times if you are advanced.

LUNGE TWIST

MANTRA: "I ascend towards joy every day."
HOLD FOR 30 SECONDS ON EACH SIDE

a) From Mountain Pose, lunge forward with your right foot.
b) Put your palms together in Prayer Position, elbows out to the side.
c) Twist your upper body to the right and place your left elbow on your knee.
d) Take 5 deep breaths.
e) Repeat on the left side.

CHAIR POSE

MANTRA: "I am sitting in the throne of light."
HOLD FOR ONE MINUTE

a) Start in Mountain Pose.
b) Inhale and raise your arms straight up next to your ears.
c) Exhale and bend your knees as if you are sitting in a chair. Try to get your thighs parallel to the floor with your bottom pushed out.
d) Lift your heart as you breathe, bringing your hips even lower (avoid lower than your knees).
e) Take 5 deep breaths.

DANCE

MANTRA: "I am free."
For one minute.

    a)   Dance however you want! Freestyle! No rules!

BALANCING TREE POSE

MANTRA: "I am balanced and ready to start my day."
HOLD FOR 30 SECONDS ON EACH SIDE

a) Stand in Mountain Pose.
b) Balance on the right leg and bend the left leg, turning the left knee out.
c) Place the sole of the left foot on the right calf or thigh. (Avoid placing the sole foot on the knee. This can produce injury).
d) Balance with your arms down or in the air. Place your hands in Prayer Position above your head.
e) Focus your eyes on one point to help you balance.
f) Take 5 deep breaths.
g) Do the opposite side.

MOUNTAIN POSE STAND

a) Stand tall with your spine and your head proud.
b) Place your feet parallel, hips' distance apart.
c) Let your arms hang loosely by your sides.

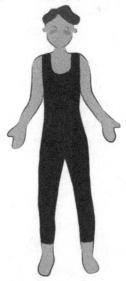

HORSE STAND

DAILY IDEAS TO BOOST HAPPINESS AND JOY

DAY 1   *MAKE A LIST OF THE THINGS THAT MAKE YOU HAPPY*

DAY 2   *SHARE SOMETHING BEAUTIFUL WITH SOMEONE*

DAY 3   *BEAUTIFY YOUR BODY*

DAY 4   *MAKE A LIST OF THE THINGS THAT MAKE YOU LAUGH*

DAY 5   *READ A BOOK*

DAY 6   *TREAT YOURSELF TO ANYTHING*

DAY 7   *DANCE FOR AT LEAST AN HOUR*

DAY 8   *GO TO (OR WATCH) A COMEDY SHOW*

DAY 9   *MAKE A LIST OF THINGS YOU ARE GRATEFUL FOR*

DAY 10   *TAKE AN EPSON SALT BATH*

DAY 11   *CONNECT WITH A PET OR AN ANIMAL*

DAY 12   *COOK SOMETHING SPECIAL FOR YOURSELF*

DAY 13   *EXPLORE A NEW PART OF THE CITY*

DAY 14   *EAT CHOCOLATE*

DAY 15   *WRITE YOUR FIRST HAPPY MEMORY DOWN*

DAY 16   *FLOAT YOUR STRESS AWAY*

DAY 17   *GO TO A CONCERT OR WATCH A MUSIC SHOW ONLINE*

DAY 18   *FORGIVE ANYONE WHO HAS BETRAYED YOU*

DAY 19 *SEND A MESSAGE OR LETTER TO SOMEONE YOU HAVEN'T TALKED TO IN A WHILE*

DAY 20 *DO BREATHING EXERCISES*

DAY 21 *GET OUT YOUR HOUSE AND VISIT A FRIEND*

DAY 22 *BUILD AN ALTAR THAT DESCRIBES WHO YOU ARE*

REFERENCES

1. American Psychological Association. *APA concise dictionary of psychology*. Washington, DC: American Psychological Association, 2009. Print.

2. (2016, June 15). 10 extremely precise words for emotions you didn't even know you had. *The Cut*. Retrieved from https://www.thecut.com/2016/06/10-extremely-precise-words-for-emotions-you-didnt-even-know-you-had.html

3. Karimova, H. (2019, April 7). The emotion wheel: What it is and how to use it. Retrieved from https://positivepsychology.com/emotion-wheel

4. Lomas, T. (2019). Provisional lexicography—By theme. Retrieved from https://www.researchgate.net/publication/332849215_Lexicography_listed_by_theme#pf2f

5. Nummenmaa, L. Glerean, E., Hari, R., & Hietanen, J. K. (2014, January 14). Bodily maps of emotions. *Proceedings of the National Academy of Sciences of the United States of America, 111*(2), 646-651.

6. Prinz, J. J. (2007). *The emotional construction of morals*. Oxford: Oxford University Press.

7. You2. A hight-Velocity Formula for Multiplying your Personal Effectiveness in Quantum Leaps. Pritchett.

8. Eat Right for your type. The individualized blood type diet solution. Dr. Peter J D'adamo.

9. How to win friends and Influence People. Dale Carnegie. Gallery Books.

10. The Atlas of Mind Body and Spirit. PaulHougham. Gaia.

11. Rockhouse, creating wealth from inside out. Master Transformational Leader & Coach Certification.

12. Wall Street Yoga. Gurunanda's happy breath yoga.

CPSIA information can be obtained
at www.ICGtesting.com
Printed in the USA
LVHW090611101120
671123LV00011BA/247